Oklahoma Native Plants

*A Guide to Designing
Landscapes to Attract
Birds and Butterflies*

Connie Scothorn, ASLA, RLA
with Brian Patric, ASLA, RLA

THE ROADRUNNER PRESS
OKLAHOMA CITY, OKLAHOMA

Copyright © 2019 by Connie Scothorn
Cover Copyright © The RoadRunner Press
Cover Photo © Ken Schulze / Shutterstock.com
Back Cover Photo © Darlene Tompkins / Shutterstock.com
Cover Design: Jeanne Devlin

Cover photo: Purple Coneflower, *Echinacea purpurea*, and Black-Eyed Susan, *Rudbeckia hirta*, in a summer garden.

The RoadRunner Press is committed to publishing works of quality and integrity. The story, the experiences, and the words shared here are the authors' alone.

All rights reserved.

The RoadRunner Press
P.O. Box 2564
Oklahoma City, OK 73101
www.TheRoadRunnerPress.com

Bulk copies or group sales of this book available by contacting orders@theroadrunnerpress.com or calling (405) 524-6205.

FIRST EDITION JUNE 2019
Printed in the USA

Library of Congress Control Number: 2019943264

ISBN: 978-1-950871-001 (trade paper)
ISBN: 978-1-950871-01-8 (eBook)

10 9 8 7 6 5 4 3 2 1

To all the gardeners who work
in the dirt and dance with flowers,
may you continue to explore our natural
landscape and protect it for future generations

Celebrating 20 years in 2019

Black-Eyed Susan *(Rudbeckia hirta)*

Table of Contents

Native Plants: A Definition 1
Introduction 3
How To Use This Book 5
Plant Hardiness Zone Maps 8
Tools 12
Forbs 15
Grasses 67
Like This, Try This 83
Preparing to Plant 85
Oklahoma Plant Chart 88
Common Questions 93
Other Native Plants to Try 95
Where to See Native Plants 97
Glossary 99
Acknowledgments 101
Resources 103
Common Name Index 104
Scientific Name Index 105
About the Authors 106

Pink Muhly Grass *(Muhlenbergia capillaris)*

A Definition

Garden as though you will live forever.
—**William Kent,**
English landscape architect

Native Plants

There is no real agreement when it comes to defining what constitutes a *native plant*, but the *Merriam-Webster* dictionary defines it like so:

> **native**: grown, produced, or originating in a particular place or in the vicinity: living or growing naturally in a particular region

For this book, we will stretch the definition to be "a plant that occurs naturally in the United States and is adapted to the Oklahoma climate." That means not all of the plants in this book are historically *native* to Oklahoma, although most are. However, we have also included several *nativars*, or cultivars of native plants that may have been selected for better flowering, color, size, or other characteristics as well as how they fare in this region.

Some people may find this definition too liberal, and we understand and respect their opinion. However, in the end, we decided to let gardeners decide for themselves. The purpose of this book is to encourage the use of native plants in the ornamental landscape—both for what native plants can add visually to the landscape but also for the good they can do once established for the environment, and so we feel this liberal interpretation is appropriate. Happy planting!

—**The Authors**

Pink Preference *(Salvia greggii)*, Oklahoma Veterans Memorial, State Capitol Park, Oklahoma City, Oklahoma

Introduction

Anyone who believes gardening is easy does not live in the state of Oklahoma, where we have wind, cold, heat, wet, and dry—sometimes all in one week, sometimes all in a single day. Only plants that have evolved to handle such unpredictable, fluctuating weather conditions can flourish here.

Yet it is the norm, not the exception, to see homes and businesses landscaped without a single native plant. In fact, most Oklahoma landscapes are covered in plants from China, Japan, Europe, and Africa. Is it any wonder that such gardens suffer and become labor intensive?

Why do Oklahomans not use more native plants in the garden? For one, people tend to plant what they know and what garden centers and seed catalogs champion. And two, many people believe that native plants only come in neutral tan and buff hues—which couldn't be further from the case.

We hope to dispel some of those myths and misconceptions about native plants with this book as we share the many reasons to use native plants, including:

1. Their beauty, with flower and leaf colors that rival any plant outside of our borders.

2. Their ability to evoke a sense of place, providing a reference to the native ecology.

3. Their adaptability to the environment, as this is where they naturally evolved. Hence, the need for maintenance, irrigation, and chemical treatments is reduced.

4. Their role in providing sustenance for native pollinator species such as birds, bees, and butterflies, all of which are declining in numbers and,

in some cases, facing extinction. Can we live without these species? Not without a significant cost. One out of every three bites of food that we eat depends on the pollination of a plant. These species also eat our pests (mosquitoes and other unfavorable insects) and provide beauty for our enjoyment.

Some believe the next world crisis will stem from dwindling water supplies, and the U.S. Agency for International Development predicts by 2025, one-third of all humans will face severe and chronic water shortages. We need to change the way we landscape our cities, parks, buildings, and homes—moving toward plants that can exist on the water naturally provided in a region while also providing sustenance for native pollinators.

This book is written from the perspective of two licensed landscape architects, both of whom care about the way our landscape looks and functions ecologically. We hope to introduce municipalities, designers, and property owners to the joys and benefits of landscaping with native plants in a way that is beautiful and supports our natural environment.

More than 2,600 native plant species grow in Oklahoma. Not all are ornamental or appropriate to use in the landscape in the traditional sense. However, those included in this book are.

Ours is not a complete list, but it comprises those plants that we are both familiar with and have had experience growing, all in the hopes that you will be inspired to include native plants in your own landscape.

How To Use This Book

Breathless, we flung us on a windy hill,
Laughed in the sun, and kissed the lovely grass.
—**Rupert Brooke,**
English poet

Using this Book

We have arranged the native plants in this book alphabetically by *botanical name* per standard horticultural practice. For ease of use, you can also find the *common name* beneath in the blue bar.

Botanical / Scientific Names

Botanical, or scientific, names are unique to specific plants, always Latin or Latinized words, and standardized, meaning they cannot be changed except by international scientific agreement.

Botanical and scientific names are used across the world by scientists and professionals. They are the industry standard because common names can be changed on the whim of the grower or landscaper, and we want to ensure that you always purchase the plant you intended.

In fact, some of the plants within this book are listed with more than one common name because their names can vary from place to place—hence, the importance of having the botanical name at the ready. Once a genus of a plant is used on a page, the genus may be abbreviated, such as *A. hubrichtii*, instead of repeating the full name: *Amsonia hubrichtii*.

Common Names

Common names for plants may vary from country to country, state to state, county to county, and even community to community.

Common names can change as new people move to a region or old common names fall out of favor. And it isn't unusual even in the same place for a plant to have more than one common name. In this book, the common names of plants will be capitalized.

Cultivar Names

Cultivars are simply variations of a plant species. They may begin as chance seedlings found in the nursery or garden that have special color or growing traits. They may also be deliberately bred for a special characteristic. Either way, the names of cultivars are designated with single quotation marks (in a punctuation departure the quotes belong inside any punctuation): Blond Ambition 'Blue Grama' with 'Blue Grama' being the cultivar name, or *Salvia greggi* 'Pink Preference', with 'Pink Preference' being the cultivar name. The cultivar name helps the buyer know a plant will produce the specific characteristics desired.

Description of Light Requirements

Full Sun: A location with more than six hours of sun per day.

Part Sun: A location that receives between four and six hours of sun per day or that receives dappled sun/shade all day.

Shade: A location that receives less than four hours of sun per day, with a preference to morning sun, rather than afternoon.

Top Twelve Plants for Butterflies

The "Top Twelve Plants for Butterflies" rankings are the work of Okies for Monarchs, a group that has identified plants that thrive in various parts of Oklahoma to support monarch butterflies. For more information about their work, please visit:
www.okiesformonarchs.org.

General Native Plant Availability

Readily Available: Usually available wherever plants are sold.

Available from Good Nurseries: Available from professional landscape nurseries.

Native Plant Growers: Usually available only from growers that specialize in growing and selling native plants.

Native Seed Growers: Available from seed producers who specialize in producing native seed. Local seed producers—those within two hundred miles—are recommended for the best success.

Native Sod Producers: Available from some sod farms that specialize in providing native sod.

Pollinator Indicator
Provides food for butterflies and other insects.

Provides food for birds.

United States Plant Hardiness Zone Map

8

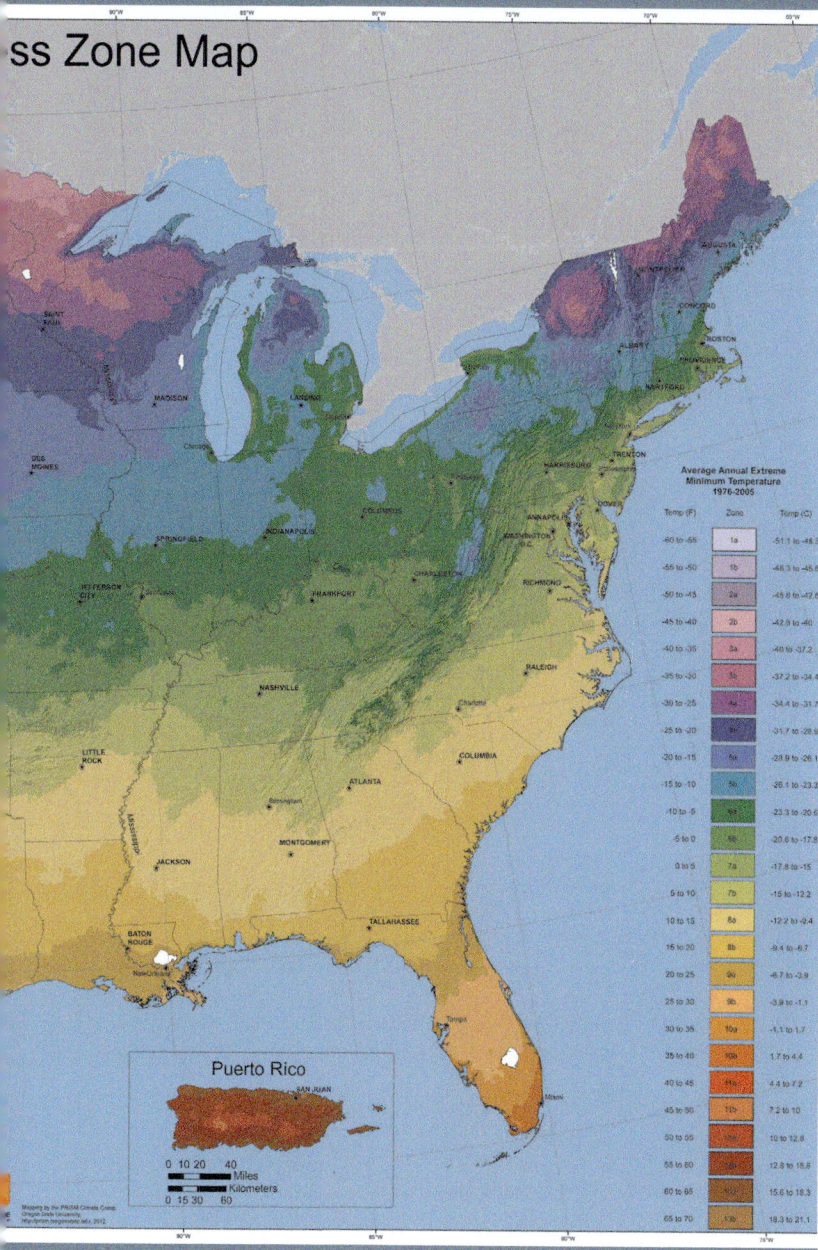

Purple Coneflower *(Echinacea purpurea)*, with a monarch butterfly

Oklahoma Hardiness Zone Map

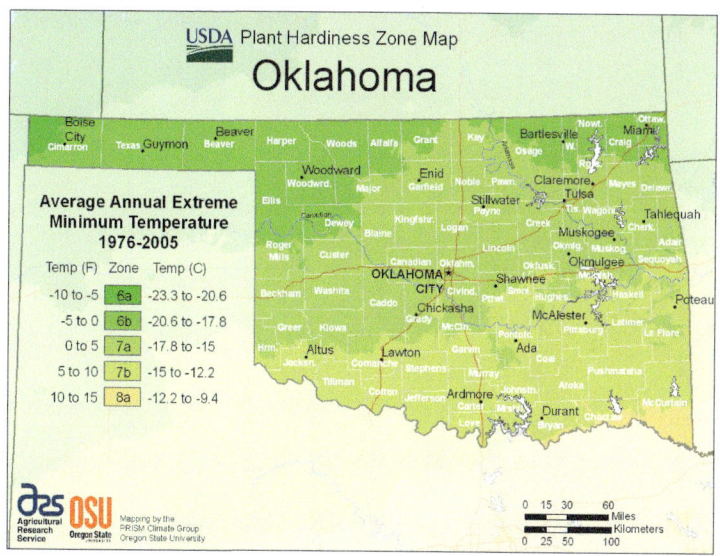

Creeping Phlox *(Phlox subulata), with rock feature*

11

A Gardener's Tools: Clockwise from hat, hand cultivator tool, gloves, sunscreen, hand pruners, shovel (with metal handle), rake, hand pruning sheers, cultivator.

Tools

All gardening is landscape painting.
—William Kent,
English landscape architect

Confessions of an Avid Gardener & Landscape Architect

You can see by the photo at the left that I do not follow the professional advice or even conventional wisdom when it comes to keeping my tools clean, oiled, and sharp.

I'm sure it would help.

But I've functioned just fine with my approach for decades.

My most indispensable tools: my hat, gloves, and sunscreen (because no one thinks they will look old until they do).

Other tools I favor: My favorite hand tool is my hand/cultivator, which is great for planting, weeding, pounding, and breaking up soil. I love it.

Other important tools include pruners, a good (not too wide) rake, a shovel (with metal handle), and a cultivator. I like brightly colored gardening tools so that you can find them easier.

Pink Creeping Phlox *(Phlox subulata)*, with an Eastern Tiger Swallowtail butterfly

Forbs

forb: *a herbaceous flowering plant other than a grass.*

Forbs are herbaceous flowering plants that are neither grasses nor woody species such as a shrub or tree.

As used in this section, the term *forb* refers to both annual and perennial plants—plants normally grown in the landscape for the enjoyment of their flower color, leaf color, and fragrance.

Forbs are important for feeding birds, bees, butterflies, and other pollinators. Many forbs also have an immense food value for livestock, including cattle, sheep, chickens, and pigs.

Yellow Yarrow *(Eriophyllum confertiflorum)*

Achillea millefolium
COMMON YARROW

Yarrow is frequently seen growing in Oklahoma meadows. With its fernlike leaves, the plant is extremely resistant to drought, especially when growing in the shade. I have found yarrow growing naturally in a shady part of my backyard without any care. The low-growing plants slowly spread by underground rhizomes and can tolerate and flower in dry shade, making yarrow especially useful in the landscape.

There are literally thousands of cultivars of yarrow in many colors including yellow, white, red, orange, and pink. Yarrow is one of the most controversial plants as to its origin—native, naturalized, or originally from Europe. I've seen all descriptions. What is indisputable is that it is beautiful and loved by native bees! Yarrow usually blooms in spring, but some plants will repeat bloom throughout the summer.

Readily Available
Size: 1-2 Feet Tall x 1-2 Feet Wide
Bloom: Many Colors / Normally Spring
Uses: Massing, Borders, Naturalizing, Ground Cover
USDA Zones: 3-9
Sun: Full Sun to Part Sun
Soil: Dry to Moist

17

Amorpha canescens
LEADPLANT

This is one tough plant! Leadplant needs absolutely no care at all and thrives in any type of soil. While it may not have the showiest of flowers, leadplant is extremely important to native bee populations. With its silvery gray foliage, leadplant can also add interest to a bed, making it a great back-of-the-border or filler plant for locations that irrigation might not reach. Leadplant is a legume so it adds nitrogen back into the soil, which makes it an excellent companion plant for other species.

The plant looks best if cut back hard in spring to maintain a more compact shape.

Fragrant False Indigo, *A. nana*, is a close relative with green leaves and growth limited to about two feet.

Available from Native Plant Growers
Size: 2-3 Feet Tall x 2-3 Feet Wide
Bloom: Purple to Blue / July to August
Uses: Naturalize, Erosion Control

USDA Zones: 2-9
Sun: Full Sun to Part Sun
Soil: Dry Sandy to Average

Amsonia (various species)
BLUESTAR

    Bluestar is a well-behaved native plant that complements any ornamental or formal landscape design. It provides delicate, fine-textured leaves with intense, pale blue, star-shaped flowers throughout spring, but it is in fall where it shines. Bluestar's stop-you-in-your-tracks yellow/gold hues in the fall add an outstanding splash of color to any yard. The plant performs best with regular irrigation and in low pH soils.

    Several other Amsonia species offer similar flowers and growth habits, including Arkansas Bluestar, *A. hubrichtii*, shown above top, which has an exquisite fine texture but is more ornamental, and Bluestar, *A. Tabernaemontana*, which has larger leaves and is a better plant for pollinators.

Available from Good Nurseries
Size: 2-3 Feet Tall x 2-3 Feet Wide
Bloom: Pale Blue / April to May
Uses: Massing, Mid Border, Accent, Rain Garden

USDA Zones: 5-8
Sun: Full Sun to Part Sun
Soil: Moist, Rich Garden Soil

Aquilegia canadensis
COLUMBINE

Even though Columbine will grow in sunny locations, the real value of this plant is its ability to grow and flower in the shade. In Oklahoma, it is definitely best to grow Columbine in the shade in rich, well-drained or moist garden soil. When temperatures reach 90 degrees Fahrenheit or higher, the plant may go dormant, unless it is watered well and protected from sun and wind.

A delicate-looking plant with beautiful flowers and small fern-like leaves, Columbine's blooms can be extended significantly with regular deadheading. Above right, Texas Cold Columbine, *A. chrysantha var. hinkleyana*, is better adapted to the Oklahoma heat and has a yellow flower. Columbine is perennial, will readily reseed and spread, and the flowers attract hummingbirds.

Available from Good Nurseries
Size: 1-3 Feet Tall x 1-3 Feet Wide
Bloom: Red, Yellow, Pink, Blue / March to April
Uses: Woodland, Shady Border, Ground Cover

USDA Zones: 3-8
Sun: Part Sun to Shade
Soil: Rich, Well-Drained, Moist Garden Soil

Asclepias syriaca
COMMON MILKWEED

If you love monarch butterflies, you must plant milkweed. The plants are vital for monarch butterflies reproduction, acting as the exclusive host plant during the butterfly's larval phase. Common Milkweed is tall, with purplish blooms, and thrives in moist soil conditions. The plant is fragrant when blooming and will self-seed year after year.

There are nearly one hundred cultivars of milkweed, and at least twenty of those are native to Oklahoma. Of those, one can be found for every type of soil, size, or bloom time. Plant a few that fit your location to help save the monarchs! Milkweed can spread by rhizomes and can be aggressive in garden soils. The plant is listed as one of the top twelve plants for butterflies.

Available from Native Plant Growers   Poisonous; Sap May Irritate Skin
Size: 2-3 Feet Tall x 1-2 Feet Wide   **USDA Zones:** 4-9
Bloom: White, Purple / June to August   **Sun:** Full Sun
Uses: Mid-Back Border, Naturalizing   **Soil:** Moist

Asclepias tuberosa
BUTTERFLY WEED

Butterfly Weed is the plant we usually think of when planting for butterflies. Compact with bright fiery-orange flowers that appear off and on throughout the summer, the plant is super easy to grow and striking when in bloom. Just remember that Butterfly Weed breaks dormancy later than most other plants in spring so don't give up on it!

When the plant starts putting out seed, it can be a little messy, but that stage is easily hidden if you plant it among other low plants. Some people say that Butterfly Weed will spread and reseed. I haven't found this to be a problem, and wouldn't mind if it did a little. Butterfly Weed, however, does not transplant easily because of its deep tap root.

The plant is listed as one of the top twelve plants for butterflies, and it is resistant to deer.

Available from Good Nurseries   Poisonous; Sap May Irritate Skin
Size: 1-2 Feet Tall x 1 Foot Wide   **USDA Zones:** 3-9
Bloom: Yellow, Orange / June to August   **Sun:** Full Sun
Uses: Naturalize, Borders, Massing   **Soil:** Dry to Medium, Well-Drained

Asclepias viridis
GREEN MILKWEED

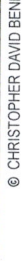
© CHRISTOPHER DAVID BENDA

Because Green Milkweed blooms earlier than other milkweeds, experts consider it one of the most important milkweeds when it comes to supporting monarch butterflies. The plant attracts monarchs on their spring migration through Oklahoma.

With its subtle purplish-white blooms and big seeds, Green Milkweed is not as showy as other milkweeds, and is best appreciated for its upright stance, which makes it a useful filler plant in the middle of a border or for naturalizing. It grows well in poor, rocky, and dry soils.

A. asperula (Antelope-Horns) is similar and more prevalent in the dry western part of the state. The value to butterflies alone makes it an important plant to use. The plant is listed as one of the top twelve plants for butterflies.

Available from Native Plant Growers   Poisonous; Sap May Irritate Skin
Size: 1-3 Feet Tall x 1-3 Feet Wide   **USDA Zones:** 3-9
Bloom: Green, with Purple Hood / April to September   **Sun:** Full Sun
Uses: Naturalize, Borders   **Soil:** Rich or Poor Soil

Baptisia australis
BLUE FALSE INDIGO

Blue False Indigo is a lovely, early-spring blooming plant with foot-long spikes of blue, pealike flowers from May to June. After flowering, the large, gray seedpods remain interesting for the rest of the year.

The plant grows best in dry to medium soils, although it can tolerate drought and poor soils. Plants grow in expanding clumps of blue-green foliage in a shrub-like habit. The plant has a deep taproot, helping to make it drought tolerant and easy to grow but also hard to transplant.

Trimming foliage after blooming will help maintain a neat plant appearance, if the seedpods aren't desired. *Baptisia* is classified in the pea family and, as with other legumes, has a symbiotic relationship with soil-dwelling bacteria that makes it capable of fixing nitrogen in the soil.

Available from Native Plant Growers
Size: 3-4 Feet Tall x 3-4 Feet Wide
Bloom: Indigo Blue / May to June
Uses: Borders, Meadow Gardens, Naturalize

USDA Zones: 3-8
Sun: Full Sun to Part Sun
Soil: Dry to Medium

Callirhoe involucrata
PURPLE POPPY MALLOW, WINECUP

Poppy Mallow is a common, spring-blooming wildflower often seen growing naturally along Oklahoma roads. With its abundant purplish-red flowers, this low-growing, sprawling ground-cover plant is not only tough but also low-maintenance. It can be used in a variety of locations, and looks great trailing over walls or mixed with other low-growing perennials. Try pairing Poppy Mallow with Black-Eyed Susan (*Rudbeckia hirta*) or other plants that bloom later in hot temperatures, because when temperatures get too hot, Poppy Mallow may go dormant and this will allow your beds to still have needed color.

Poppy Mallow has a deep tuberous taproot, which makes it drought tolerant. If irrigated well, the plant will bloom all summer.

Available from Native Plant Growers
Size: 6-12 Inches Tall x 3 Feet Wide
Bloom: Magenta / April to May
Uses: Ground Cover, Rock Garden, Border Front
USDA Zones: 3-8
Sun: Full Sun to Part Sun
Soil: Sandy, Loam, Clay

Conoclinium coelestinum
BLUE MISTFLOWER

Blue Mistflower attracts both bees and butterflies, and in my own backyard, I have seen as many as a dozen monarch butterflies at a single time covering my small four-square-foot patch of Blue Mistflower plants. When the butterflies come through on their fall migration, they stop and feast on the nectar of the plentiful blue flowers.

Blue Mistflower boasts a bluish-violet bloom that protrudes approximately a foot above the foliage. The plant tolerates both shade and sunny locations, but I find its value to be in the shade where we always need more flowering plants. Blue Mistflower spreads by underground roots but not invasively in shady locations. It can be somewhat invasive in sunny areas but is easily pulled up.

Available from Native Plant Growers
Size: 1-3 Feet Tall x 1 Foot Wide
Bloom: Blue, Purple / July to November
Uses: Ground Cover, Shade Garden

USDA Zones: 5-10
Sun: Full Sun to Shade
Soil: Any

Coreopsis lanceolata
LANCELEAF COREOPSIS

When I moved into my home, I had these little yellow flowering plants pop up each spring and quickly take over any free space in my new garden. I let them flower and appreciated the free plants. Then, after the flowering finished, I would remove them all—not anymore. Now, I mostly leave the prolific bloomers in place as a ground cover between my other perennials and grasses. Coreopsis will spread but is easily controlled.

The plant blooms for several weeks each spring with two- to three-inch-long yellow rays of petals encircling a greenish-yellow disk. Deadheading will extend bloom time significantly. Loved by bees, butterflies, and people, Coreopsis reseeds and can often be seen growing naturally along Oklahoma roadways. A low-maintenance, evergreen plant, it is very easy to grow.

Available from Good Nurseries
Size: 1-2 Feet Tall x 1-2 Feet Wide
Bloom: Yellow / May to July
Uses: Ground Cover, Massing, Naturalizing

USDA Zones: 4-9
Sun: Full Sun to Part Sun
Soil: Any

Coreopsis tripteris
TALL COREOPSIS

As its name implies, Tall Coreopsis is a towering plant that can reach six-feet in height in the partial sun area of my garden, blooming just as Large Coneflower, *Rudbeckia maxima*, finishes. That makes them great companion plants, extending the yellow bloom period and structurally supporting each other's tall foliage. Butterflies love the flowers and the birds gorge on the seeds, so don't be in a rush to cut those seed heads down. I usually wait until the following spring. Division of the plant every two to three years is recommended, but I haven't found it necessary in the four years I have enjoyed this beautiful, low-maintenance, durable plant. Coreopsis is very tolerant of heat, humidity, and drought.

It is listed as one of the top twelve plants for butterflies too.

Available from Native Plant Growers
Size: 3-6 Feet Tall x 2-3 Feet Wide
Bloom: Yellow, Orange / July to September
Uses: Accent, Massing, Rock Gardens

USDA Zones: 3-8
Sun: Full Sun to Part Sun
Soil: Dry to Medium

Coreopsis verticillata
THREADLEAF COREOPSIS

Threadleaf Coreopsis comes in several varieties with different names and colors, and I am grouping them together here. All are cultivars of native tickseed in the sunflower family, including 'Tweety', 'Moonbeam' (top photo), and 'Pink', among others. The plants are low-growing, compact, with a fine texture. Don't let their dainty form fool you, however, as they are tough bloomers and give back to birds and butterflies. The plants bloom for a long period and spread by rhizomes in the soil. Like other Coreopsis, they are tolerant of heat, humidity, and drought.

Shearing plants mid-year will promote a second flush of blooms come fall. Plants respond well to being divided every three to four years to increase vigor and to obtain additional plants.

Readily Available
Size: 2-3 Feet Tall x 2 Feet Wide
Bloom: Yellow, Orange, Pink / July to September
Uses: Accent, Borders, Massing, Rock Gardens

USDA Zones: 3-9
Sun: Full Sun
Soil: Dry to Medium

Dalea purpurea
PURPLE PRAIRIE CLOVER

Purple Prairie Clover is an easily grown, low-maintenance plant with striking purple/rose flowers. The fine textured plant has tiny purple flowers with golden flecks on a cone-like flower head. The flower's bloom begins at the bottom of the flower head and gradually moves upward as the season progresses. The bloom period lasts about a month.

Purple Prairie Clover has a deep taproot, which makes it very drought tolerant and difficult to transplant. The plant is naturally found in rocky, well-drained prairies, and does not fare well in heavy clay soils.

A nitrogen-fixing legume, it makes a lovely companion to other plants in the garden and may self-seed in good conditions. Purple Prairie Clover provides nectar to many species of butterflies and bees, and can act as a natural soil fertilizer when the spent plant is left to enrich the soil.

Available from Native Plant Growers
Size: 1-3 Feet Tall x 1-2 Feet Wide
Bloom: Rose/Purple / June to August
Uses: Border, Massing, Naturalize

USDA Zones: 3-8
Sun: Full Sun
Soil: Average, Well-Drained

Echinacea purpurea
PURPLE CONEFLOWER

There are hundreds of different species of Coneflower with hundreds of cultivars, including an array of flower colors ranging from white to purple in heights that range from two feet tall to five feet in height. The flower itself is quite distinct, with a large, rust-colored conical disk in the center topping colorful, drooping petals. After the petals drop, the centers stay until the seeds ripen, which makes the plant attractive until the fall.

A fantastic full-sun plant, the Coneflower also tolerates and flowers in shade. Its wide range of heights makes the plant a good option for borders as well as large meadow plantings. The plant grows so easily; just sow seeds directly into the garden in early spring or late fall.

Coneflower is listed as one of the top twelve plants for butterflies.

Available from Good Nurseries
Size: 2-5 Feet Tall x 1-2 Feet Wide
Bloom: White, Purple, Pink / June to August
Uses: Accent, Border, Ground Cover, Naturalize

USDA Zones: 3-8
Sun: Full Sun to Shade
Soil: Any

Engelmannia pinnatifida

ENGELMANN'S DAISY, CUTLEAF DAISY

Engelmann's Daisy is one of the most adaptable plants native to Oklahoma, thriving in almost any soil condition and in all light conditions, save for deep shade. I can vouch for its durability, low-maintenance, and drought tolerance as I planted this very daisy at my father's house and—despite his never watering it—the plant thrived for years. Delicate, yellow daisies bloom through the summer, and it produces new plants from seed. One year, I decided that I needed some of these plants for my own garden, but even the smallest seedlings had such a deep taproot I couldn't obtain a good transplant. Deadheading the flowers will extend the blooming season, and birds relish the seeds. Cattle, sheep, and goats find it so tasty this daisy is rarely found in pastures but it is resistant to deer and rabbits. The plant will flop over if soil is too rich.

Available from Native Plant Growers
Size: 1-3 Feet Tall x 1-2 Feet Wide
Bloom: Yellow / April to August
Uses: Accent, Mid-Back Border, Naturalize

USDA Zones: 5-10
Sun: Full Sun to Part Sun
Soil: Any

Eryngium yuccifolium
RATTLESNAKE MASTER

Rattlesnake Master has such an unusual flower one might think its common name stems from its spiky bloom—but no. Historic lore cites the use of the plant's sap as a treatment for rattlesnake bites, though no evidence exists for its prevention or treatment of any medical condition. Native Americans, however, did use the fibrous leaves for weaving baskets. The plant's large, sword-shaped leaves resemble those of the yucca, while the thistle-like flower heads attract small native bees, soldier beetles, and butterflies, as well as bees, wasps, and flies. The thick hollow stems double as nesting sites for tunnel-nesting bees. The plant has a taproot, making it drought tolerant and difficult to transplant.

A member of the carrot family, the plant is listed as one of the top twelve plants for butterflies.

Available from Native Plant Growers
Size: 4-5 Feet Tall x 2-3 Feet Wide
Bloom: Greenish White / June to September
Uses: Accent, Naturalize, Meadow

USDA Zones: 3-8
Sun: Full Sun
Soil: Prefers Dry, Tolerates Any

Eutrochium purpureum
SWEET JOE PYE WEED

The unique common names of plants have always intrigued me, but it took several years to locate the fragrant Joe Pye Weed, which is named after a Native American herbalist. This wildflower native can reach eight feet in height in Oklahoma and adds texture to a garden, while creating a colorful backdrop for small plants. Joe Pye Weed has tiny, pinkish purple flowers in large compound blooms and, since it blooms mid-summer, is ideal for attracting migrating butterflies. In some plants, the leaves and flowers give off a vanilla scent when crushed, and the roots and dried flowers make for a pleasant tea. Baby Joe Pye, *E. dubium* Baby Joe, is a dwarf version of the plant, topping out at just two or three feet. Both plants prefer some irrigation to perform best, or you might consider locating them on the edge of a stream or pond to ensure enough moisture.

Available from Native Plant Growers **USDA Zones:** 3-8
Size: 5-8 Feet Tall x 3-4 Feet Wide   **Sun:** Full Sun to Part Sun
Bloom: White, Pink, Purple / July to September   **Soil:** Wet to Medium-Wet, Tolerates Clay
Uses: Massing, Naturalize, Rain or Woodland Garden

Fragaria virginiana
WILD STRAWBERRY

Wild Strawberry makes for a nice, low-growing ground cover. I had a large patch of Wild Strawberry growing on the north side of my house when I moved in. At the time I found it too aggressive, so I removed it, which was a big mistake. Apparently, Wild Strawberry is that rare plant that loves shade and lousy clay soil such as I have. How I want it back!

A nice, neat plant, which looks just like the strawberry plant you plant for fruit, Wild Strawberry produces small, white flowers followed by small, tart, edible berries in summer. The value of this plant is as a ground cover thick enough to choke out weeds and yet still beautiful.

Wild Strawberry, a member of the rose family, attracts birds, butterflies, and wildlife, and it can tolerate deer, drought, erosion, and mildly acidic soil.

Available from Native Plant Growers
Size: 6 Inches Tall / Plant Twelve Inches on Center
Bloom: White / April to June
Uses: Spreading Ground Cover
USDA Zones: 5-9
Sun: Full Sun to Shade
Soil: Any

Gaillardia pulchella
INDIAN BLANKET

The state wildflower of Oklahoma since 1986, Indian Blanket adds bold, fiery color to the summer garden or meadow. A tough and extremely showy member of the daisy family, the plant includes many cultivars with double flowering and color options.

An annual plant also known as Firewheel, it is easily grown in full sun and sandy, rocky soils. Rich soils will actually produce tall, floppy plants.

Sow the seeds directly into the garden either in the fall or after the last spring frost. Prolong the bloom period by deadheading, but be sure to leave some spent flowerheads for the birds to eat. Indian Blanket will reseed in optimal conditions. A lovely cut flower, the plant is loved by native bees and butterflies.

Available: Native Seed Producers, Native Plant Growers   **USDA Zones:** 2-10
Size: 12-24 Inches Tall x 12 Inches Wide   **Sun:** Full Sun
Bloom: Red Center, Yellow Fringe / May to August   **Soil:** Dry to Medium
Uses: Annuals, Naturalizing, Borders, Rock Gardens

Gaura lindheimeri

GAURA

Native Gaura is an extremely tough, drought-tolerant plant that blooms all summer with the daintiest of flowers. A member of the evening primrose family, the deep-rooted plant has a taproot that can make it difficult to transplant Gaura after only a year.

Also known as Wandflower and Whirling Butterfly for the way the small flowers dance amongst the long, pinkish stems, the plant's wayward stems can be cut back to maintain shape and promote new flowering. As with all plants, it is important to put Gaura in the right spot in order to avoid excessive pruning of flower buds.

'Siskiyou Pink' is a more compact, hardy pink cultivar that is much showier than the standard white.

Available from Good Nurseries
Size: 2-4 Feet Tall x 2-4 Feet Wide
Bloom: White, Pink / May to September
Uses: Accent, Borders, Massing, Rock Gardens

USDA Zones: 5-9
Sun: Full Sun
Soil: Dry to Medium

Helianthus maximiliani
MAXIMILIAN SUNFLOWER

Maximilian Sunflower can reach ten feet in height—more than two feet taller than the tallest player ever in the NBA! Large flowers start in late summer and extend into the fall, with the plant reaching its fullest potential in moist ditches in full sun. Still, even in drought-plagued locations, it can grow to be four feet tall. A native prairie perennial, also known as Prairie Sunflower, it produces a heavy seed crop, providing needed forage for livestock, goldfinches, and other wildlife.

A fun fact: Squirrels find the plants difficult to climb so unlike other sunflowers the birds, not the squirrels, usually get the seeds. The plant can be messy at the base so it is best planted in the back of the border or behind lower grasses. If planted in overly fertile soil the plants may need to be staked prior to flowering. It spreads via rhizomes.

Available from Native Plant Growers
Size: 6-10 Feet Tall x 3 Feet Wide
Bloom: Yellow, with Orange Center / August to October
Uses: Accent, Back Border, Mass Plantings
USDA Zones: 3-8
Sun: Full Sun to Part Sun
Soil: Any

Heliopsis helianthoides
FALSE SUNFLOWER

© CHRISTOPHER DAVID BENDA

False Sunflower provides a long, summer bloom and works well as part of a naturalized area or prairie setting. This perennial is remarkably easy to grow with drought-tolerant characteristics, and has attractive sunflower-like flowers, with orange-yellow rays shooting out of brown center disks.

The plant needs staking in order to stay upright. Alternately, the stems can be cut back by one-third to one-half in May to reduce the height of the plant. If left at its full height, False Sunflower is a wonderful plant for cut flowers, and no matter its height, the plant will attract hummingbirds.

Available from Native Plant Growers
Size: 3-6 Feet Tall x 2-4 Feet Wide
Bloom: Orange-Yellow, Brown Center / June to August
Uses: Back Border, Cut Flower, Naturalized

USDA Zones: 3-9
Sun: Full Sun
Soil: Any

Heuchera americana
HEUCHERA, CORAL BELLS, ALUMNROOT

    A mounding evergreen perennial wildflower, Heuchera, or Coral Bells, thrives in moist rich woods in shade to partial sun, and while its flower displays are not often showy, they do provide a light texture to landscapes. Cultivars display colorful evergreen leaves that remind me of the annual Coleus plant. Foliage in red, purple, lime, peach, green, or silvery green makes a striking statement even without flowers. However, the cultivars seem to possess less vigor.

    The pink, red, or white flower clusters at the end of tall, wiry stalks can extend fifteen inches above the base of the plant. Despite being natives and nativars, the plants require a higher level of maintenance, including protection from the sun, good air circulation to prevent diseases, winter mulching, rich soils, and perfect drainage.

Readily Available
Size: 1-2 Feet Tall x 1-2 Feet Wide
Bloom: Greenish-White / June to August
Uses: Ground Cover, Rock Garden, Raised Beds

USDA Zones: 4-9
Sun: Full Sun to Part Sun
Soil: Organically Rich Moist, Well-Drained

Liatris (various species)
BLAZING STAR, GAYFEATHER

Gayfeather is a showy native plant with flowers that look like purple exclamation marks; flowers last from late summer through early fall. Similar to other fall-blooming plants, Gayfeather is like candy to monarchs on their fall migration. It is listed as one of the top twelve plants for butterflies.

The plant is easy to grow and can be a long-lasting addition to the garden as long as soil is well-drained. It looks and performs best when planted in groups of three or more. *Liatris* may be grown from seed, but it is slow to establish.

'Kobold' is a lower-growing cultivar that tops out at about two-feet tall, and so does not need staking. Other species of *Liatris* are worth considering for different sizes. Both *L. aspera* (two to three feet tall) and *L. pycnostachya* (two to five feet tall) love poor, sandy soils.

Available from Good Nurseries
Size: 2-5 Feet Tall x 1-2 Feet Wide
Bloom: Rose-Purple / August to October
Uses: Accent, Border, Cut Flowers, Massing, Rock Garden

USDA Zones: 3-9
Sun: Full Sun
Soil: Well-Drained

Lobelia cardinalis
CARDINAL FLOWER

Gardens frequently have a place that is wet and swampy with poor drainage where nothing grows. That spot is ideal for Cardinal Flower, which may be the perfect water garden plant. It must be sited carefully—along streams, ponds, springs, and in low damp wooded areas. Soil around Cardinal plants should be kept moist at all times, and the plant will even tolerate flooding for brief periods.

The showy, eight-inch-long flower spikes feature bright red terminal flowers that attract hummingbirds (necessary for pollinating this plant in late summer and early fall). Best grown where it gets morning sun and afternoon shade, it also benefits from mulching that helps hold moisture. The short-lived perennial can be propagated by bending and fastening a stem into the mud.

Available from Native Plant Growers
Size: 2-4 Feet Tall x 1-2 Feet Wide
Bloom: Red / July to September
Uses: Naturalize, Near Ponds/Streams, Water Garden

All plant parts toxic if swallowed.
USDA Zones: 3-9
Sun: Full Sun to Part Sun
Soil: Moist

Malvaviscus arboreus
TURK'S CAP

True red flowers are unusual to find in nature but Turk's Cap, also known as Ladies's Eardrops, Scotchman's Purse, and Wild Fuchsia, has them. Blooms are small but numerous, with swirled petals that always look about to open but never do. The plant's bright red color attracts and pleases the eye. Turk's Cap blooms through the summer heat and into the cool of fall, with mounded foliage that attracts butterflies, bees, and hummingbirds—yet is resistant to damage by deer. Its leaves can span five inches, making for a stark contrast to the tiny flowers.

Turk's Cap usually freezes back to the ground during harsh winters. When this happens, cut back and remove all dead materials, and new shoots will emerge the following spring. Actually, even without a freeze, it is still a good idea to cut the plant back to encourage new growth.

Available from Native Plant Growers
Size: 3-6 Feet Tall x 3 Feet Wide
Bloom: Red / July to September
Uses: Mid-Back Border, Shade, Wetland

USDA Zones: 7-11
Sun: Sun to Full Shade
Soil: Woodland, Tolerant Drought, Sandy, Clay

Melampodium leucanthum
BLACKFOOT DAISY

A charming, long-blooming plant with showy white flowers that last throughout the growing season, Blackfoot Daisy is often sold as a perennial. However, in my experience, it is best used as an annual because it is a finicky plant that sometimes comes back and sometimes does not. When it does come back, it may not even return in the same place where it was originally planted.

The plant grows neatly, spreads as much as two to three feet, and boasts tiny daisy-like flowers throughout the season. Blackfoot Daisy is drought-tolerant, deer resistant, and virtually maintenance free. With its honey-scented flower heads, Blackfoot Daisy, or Rock Daisy as it is also known, is a worthwhile plant, even if it lasts only a year in your yard.

Available from Native Plant Growers
Size: 8-12 Inches Tall x 24 Inches Wide
Bloom: White, Yellow Center / March to November
Uses: Ground Cover, Rock Garden

USDA Zones: 4-8
Sun: Full Sun
Soil: Limestone, Sand, Well-Drained

Monarda fistulosa
BEE BALM

    The flowers of the Bee Balm plant are strikingly interesting and include an open, daisy-like shape with extruding tubular petals of pink or purple. As with other members of the mint family, what appears to be a large single flower is actually a cluster of small blossoms—perfectly designed for butterflies and hummingbirds. Bee Balm has a size that makes it best suited for a back-of-the-border planting that also covers the feet of the plant, which can get somewhat leggy. The plant is susceptible to several diseases including powdery mildew, but should do well in marshy areas or along stream banks.

    Bee Balm should be deadheaded to prolong the bloom period and to prevent self-seeding. Many cultivars are available including dwarfs and mildew-resistant selections.

Available from Native Plant Growers
Size: 2-4 Feet Tall x 2-3 Feet Wide
Bloom: Lavender, Pink / July to September
Uses: Accent, Back Border, Naturalize, Rain Garden

USDA Zones: 4-9
Sun: Full Sun to Part Sun
Soil: Rich, Moisture-Retentive

Packera obovata
GOLDEN RAGWORT

Golden Ragwort makes a beautiful ground cover that thrives and blooms in deep shade. Its long bloom time begins in early spring, about the same time as the dogwoods bloom. Flat-topped clusters of bright yellow, daisy-like flowers grow on stems one- to two-inches above the plant. For the rest of the year, the plant makes a beautiful, low-growing, four- to six-inch, evergreen ground cover as long as some moisture is present.

Golden Ragwort will spread, and some might even call it invasive, so placement is important. Once established, the plant naturalizes into large colonies by reseeding and through stolons, or runners.

Most animals shun the foliage as it is toxic, although sheep are known to eat it. A member of the aster family, its roots and leaves were traditionally used by Native American in medicinal teas.

Available from Native Plant Growers
Size: 1-1.5 Feet Tall x 1 Feet Wide
Bloom: Yellow / April to May
Uses: Ground Cover, Naturalize, Rain Garden

USDA Zones: 3-8
Sun: Full Sun to Shade
Soil: Moist, Well-Drained

Penstemon digitalis
BEARD TONGUE

Penstemon is a genus of about 250 species of herbaceous perennials that live in a variety of habitats ranging from desert to mountain slopes, and many hybrids of this plant have been developed over the years. Its scientific name references the Latin *digitus*, or finger, for its flowers that can look like the fingers of a glove.

Beard Tongue is a great bloomer for clay loam and in areas with poor drainage. It grows well in full sun but will tolerate dry shade which is an immense bonus. Among the many cultivars of *Penstemon* are 'Dark Towers', which has pale pink flowers and dark wine-red foliage. The foliage stands out throughout the growing season. For a neat appearance, cut spent bloom stalks after flowering. Root rot can be a problem in wet, poorly drained soils.

Available from Native Plant Growers
Size: 3-5 Feet Tall x 1.5-2 Feet Wide
Bloom: White / May to July
Uses: Accent, Borders, Cottage Gardens

USDA Zones: 3-8
Sun: Full Sun to Part Sun
Soil: Dry to Wet, Clay Loam

47

Phlox divaricata
WILD BLUE PHLOX

A woodland phlox of great value, Wild Blue Phlox grows and blooms well in part sun to shady areas. Also known as Woodland Phlox, the fragrant wildflower is often found in woods with rich soils and along streams.

In the spring, Wild Blue Phlox is covered with beautiful, slightly fragrant and showy blue flowers. The plant can spread and form colonies as stems along the ground take root. However, Wild Blue Phlox is not overly aggressive, and unwanted seedlings are easily pulled, or even better, transplanted.

Cutting back stems after flowering can help control powdery mildew in Wild Blue Phlox. The plant draws little interest from deer, although the same can not be said for rabbits.

Available from Native Plant Growers
Size: 8-12 Inches Tall x 8-12 Inches Wide
Bloom: Rose/Lavendar, Violet/Blue / April to May
Uses: Ground Cover, Shady Border, Woodland

USDA Zones: 2-10
Sun: Part Sun to Shade
Soil: Rich, Well-Drained, Moist

Phlox paniculata
TALL GARDEN PHLOX

Surprisingly, Tall Garden Phlox is the very same old-fashioned phlox your grandmother kept in her garden. Who knew it was native to Oklahoma! The plant spreads in wet locations but is not difficult to control. It will also grow in sun and partial shade as well as in rich garden soil, although it does require regular watering so it is not a plant for dry areas. All of the varieties of garden phlox that I have grown have been from divisions from a friend or neighbor.

Many cultivars are available in a variety of flower colors, including white, lavender, pink, rose, red, and attractive bicolored flowers. Cultivars resistant to powdery mildew should be selected, as that can be a problem. Flowers are quite fragrant. Some of the taller cultivars may need staking.

Readily Available
Size: 2-4 Feet Tall x 2-3 Feet Wide
Bloom: Pink, Purple, White / July to September
Uses: Naturalizing Wet Sites, Border, Shade Gardens
USDA Zones: 4-8
Sun: Full Sun to Part Sun
Soil: Well-Drained, Medium Moist

49

Phlox pilosa
DOWNY PHLOX, PRAIRIE PHLOX

© CHRISTOPHER DAVID BENDA

Prairie Phlox has fragrant, tubular, one-half-inch long pink to pale purple flowers loosely packed in clusters. Butterflies and bees love the intensely fragrant flowers that bloom for about three to four weeks in the early spring. The flowers are designed perfectly for butterflies with wide petals and a long narrow corolla. Often called Downy Phlox because of the hairy-like appearance of its stems and leaves, the plant has a taproot that sends up several stems from the same root system. The plant can have problems with spider mites in hot, dry locations but is deer resistant.

The cultivar 'Eco Happy Traveler' will bloom much longer than the regular *Pilosa*. Fruits can open quickly, so if you want to save the seed try tying a mesh bag around the developing fruit.

Available from Native Plant Growers
Size: 1-2 Feet Tall x 1-1.5 Feet Wide
Bloom: Pink to Pale Purple / May to June
Uses: Borders, Prairie, Rock Gardens, Wild Gardens
USDA Zones: 4-9
Sun: Full Sun to Part Sun
Soil: Sandy, Rocky Loam, Well-Drained

Phlox subulata
CREEPING PHLOX

A familiar, creeping plant, Creeping Phlox bursts into flower about the same time as spring bulbs, making its blooms one of the earliest signs that spring has arrived. Flowers carpet the plant and last about two to four weeks.

A common ornamental ground cover, the plant comes in a multitude of flower colors, including red, white, blue, rose, lavender, or pink. After the bloom disappears, the leaves remain green, although somewhat subdued, for most of the year. Creeping Phlox has needlelike foliage and is tolerant of summer drought, heat, and compacted soils.

To promote more dense growth, cut back the stems of the plant after it flowers.

Readily Available
Size: 4-8 Inches Tall x 12-24 Inches Wide
Bloom: Blue, Pink, Red / March to April
Uses: Border Edges, Ground Cover, Rock Gardens

USDA Zones: 3-9
Sun: Full Sun
Soil: Well-Drained Rich or Sandy

Phyla nodiflora
FROGFRUIT

Another well-named plant, Frogfruit is a remarkable low-growing ground cover with miniature flowers just about the right size to be appreciated by the frog. It flourishes in partial shade, and the tiny blooms attract tiny bees as well as butterflies.

Frogfruit prefers damp areas. However, it also grows well in dry shade, one of the harshest environments for any plant. Frogfruit can spread to cover a large area and is appropriately used under large, existing trees or open spaces where it will have room to grow. The plant does not take foot traffic well. Although the flowers are small, it flowers most of the year, and is evergreen in warm years. It can tolerate drought and flooding, and attracts insect pollinators and butterflies.

Available from Native Plant Growers
Size: 3-10 Inches Tall x 2 Feet Wide
Bloom: White / April to October
Uses: Ground Cover, Hanging Baskets

USDA Zones: 6-10
Sun: Full Sun to Part Sun
Soil: Any

Pycnanthemum tenuifolium
SLENDER MOUNTAIN MINT

Mountain Mint grows well in dry areas, clay soil, and even in rocky soils—and that is a plus. The plant has silvery foliage and showy white flowers loved by bees and butterflies, and its flowers and leaves emit a pleasant minty scent when crushed.

An easily grown, upright, shrubby perennial plant, Mountain Mint can be vigorous and maybe even aggressive, so again, placement is important. Deer may browse the leaves, and various animals will eat the seeds, although the seeds are too small to attract birds. Leaves rubbed on your skin are said to repel mosquitoes, and the plant spreads quickly via rhizomes, making it a fine soil stabilizer. *P. tenuifolium* also goes by the names Common Horsemint and Narrowleaf Mountain Mint.

Available from Native Plant Growers
Size: 2-3 Feet Tall x 2-3 Feet Wide
Bloom: White / July to September
Uses: Cut Flowers, Naturalize, Rain Garden

USDA Zones: 4-8
Sun: Full Sun to Part Sun
Soil: Any

Ratabida columnifera
MEXICAN HAT

Mexican Hat takes its name from the distinctive shape of the flower, which looks something like a small sombrero. The tall, leafless flower stalk can reach three feet tall, although it is more likely to top out at about half that height. The plant blooms from May to July, but blooms can extend through September if there is plenty of moisture. The rest of the year the foliage is light, lacy, and attractive.

A fast-growing wildflower, Mexican Hat is not fussy about soils and is easy to grow from seed. Success will be seen most often if seeds are planted in fall, although they may be seeded in spring. The plant is frequently seeded into lawns and on the side of the highway, thriving so long as it has good seed-to-soil contact. Mexican Hat is perennial, but a harsh winter may kill it off. It has a deep taproot, making it very drought tolerant.

Available from Native Plant Growers
Size: 1-3 Feet Tall x 1 Foot Wide
Bloom: Yellow, Orange / May to August
Uses: Border Front, Massing, Naturalize

USDA Zones: 3-9
Sun: Full Sun
Soil: Dry to Medium Well-Drained

Rudbeckia hirta

BLACK-EYED SUSAN

A member of the aster family, Black-Eyed Susans usually have thirteen petals that have come to symbolize for many the thirteen original American colonies. One thing is for certain: When the plant is in bloom, you can't miss it. It looks just like its name: an outstanding yellow-gold bloom with a black-eyed center. Black-Eyed Susan blooms continually through the summer months and will seed, spread, and overtake some smaller plants. So, placement is important.

Several species and cultivars offer different colors and sizes, and you can easily grow the plant by sowing the seeds directly into the garden after the last spring frost. The plant is highly drought- and heat-tolerant. Native Americans used it in treatment of the common cold, flu, snake bites, and earaches.

Available from Good Nurseries
Size: 2-3 Feet Tall x 1-2 Feet Wide
Bloom: Orange, Yellow with Black Center / June to September
Uses: Cut Flowers, Ground Cover, Massing, Meadows

USDA Zones: 3-7
Sun: Sun to Part Sun
Soil: All But Poorly Drained, Best Sandy

Rudbeckia maxima
GIANT CONEFLOWER

Giant Coneflower is the plant that my neighbors ask me about most often. Big and showy, the plant easily reaches six feet tall when in bloom. Large, grayish-green leaves remain interesting for most of the growing season. The seed heads stay showy well into the winter, providing a seed source for the goldfinches and maintaining a structure in the landscape when other plants aren't doing much. So resist cutting the seed heads back until the following spring. The plant creates a real focal point in the landscape and makes a good companion plant to Tall Coreopsis, *Coreopsis tripteris*, which has a similar height and flower color.

The plant is pest resistant and foliage is unpalatable to deer and other herbivores. It was discovered by the English botanist Thomas Nuttall in 1816 near the Red River in what was then Oklahoma Territory.

Available from Native Plant Growers
Size: 5-7 Feet Tall x 3-4 Feet Wide
Bloom: Yellow with Brown Center / June to July
Uses: Accent, Back Border, Cut Flower

USDA Zones: 4-9
Sun: Full Sun to Part Sun
Soil: Tolerates Most, Best in Well-Drained, Rich

Rudbeckia submentosa
SWEET CONEFLOWER

Sweet Coneflower offers a dazzling display of golden yellow flowers with dark brown, dome-shaped centers in the mid-summer—making this plant a native superstar. Plants are long-lived and resilient. It flowers in late summer, between the seasons of many other flowering plants. Foliage is medium green in a tidy basal clump from which the strong, multiples of flowering stems arise.

An upright perennial that can reach nearly six feet in height, Sweet Coneflower can topple over if spoiled by too much water or fertilizer. Also known as Fragrant Coneflower, its yellow daisy-like flowers emit a faint, sweet, anise-like scent. The Sweet Coneflower is more long-lived than its sisters, Black-Eyed Susan and Brown-Eyed Susan.

Available from Native Plant Growers
Size: 5-7 Feet Tall x 3-4 Feet Wide
Bloom: Yellow with Brown Center / June to July
Uses: Accent, Borders, Naturalize, Rain Garden
USDA Zones: 4-9
Sun: Full Sun to Part Sun
Soil: Moist to Wet, Clay

Salvia greggii
AUTUMN SAGE

    I loved this plant before I knew it was a native and before I understood the importance of providing for our pollinators. Autumn Sage is a beautifully compact and well-behaved plant that starts blooming in spring and reaches a crescendo in the fall, hence its name, Autumn Sage.

    Salvia greggi comes in many colors: white, salmon, peppermint, purple, and orange; however, the 'Pink Preference' cultivar is preferred for its colorful pink-red flowers that, unlike other colors, last a full season. The only maintenance required for this plant is to cut it back to about a foot tall in the early spring, which allows it to maintain a neat shape at two- to three-feet tall throughout the year. Hummingbirds absolutely love this plant and can frequently be seen hovering around, grabbing some of the plant's ample and sweet nectar.

Readily Available
Size: 1-3 Feet Tall x 3 Feet Wide
Bloom: Orange, Pink-Red, Purple, White / March to November
Uses: Accent, Herb Garden, Mid-Border, Foundation Shrub
USDA Zones: 5-9
Sun: Full Sun
Soil: Well-Drained

Silphium perfoliatum

CUP PLANT

Cup Plant is a coarse, sunflower-like native plant that naturally occurs in woodlands and thickets, meadows, and near streams or ponds. Tall, with cup-forming leaves that hold water and attract birds and frogs, the plant is best suited to wet areas and partial shade, although it will tolerate some drought once established. Grandiose flowers grow as large as three- to four-inches in diameter—yellow with dark yellow centers.

If the plant likes its location, it will reseed and spread, popping up everywhere in the landscape. Cup Plant needs very little care, and that makes it work nicely for a back-of-the-border planting. The plant attracts a high number of bees of all kinds and blooms into September.

Available from Native Plant Growers
Size: 4-8 Feet Tall x 1-3 Feet Wide
Bloom: Yellow, Dark Center / July to September
Uses: Back Border, Meadows, Naturalize, Rain Garden

USDA Zones: 3-9
Sun: Full Sun
Soil: Clay or Wet

59

Solidago (various species)
GOLDENROD

    Goldenrod will stop traffic in the fall when it is completely covered with foot-long, bright yellow-gold blooms. The most common species can reach almost five-feet tall and four-feet wide; other cultivars may top out a little shorter or taller. I have the compact, well-behaved cultivar 'Wichita Mountains' in my landscape and it tops out at about two-feet tall.

    The plant is quite easy to grow, tolerant of a wide range of soils, heat, drought, and frost. There are more than a hundred species of Goldenrod, many native to the United States. Most of them prefer dry sun but look for species that match your soil condition, sun exposure, and desired size. The plant has a bad rap as the cause for fall hay fever, but it just happens to bloom at the same time as ragweed, the actual cause. Goldenrod is one of the top twelve plants for butterflies.

Available from Native Plant Growers
Size: 2-5 Feet Tall x 2-3 Feet Wide
Bloom: Yellow-Gold / July to November
Uses: Accent, Border, Massing
USDA Zones: 3-8
Sun: Full Sun
Soil: Dry to Moderately Moist, Well-Drained

Symphyotrichum (various species)
AROMATIC ASTER

Asters do not do much for most of the year, but then along comes September, and those quiet little green shrubs turn a bright purple with one- to two-inch-wide flowers covering the entire plant. Asters provide far better fall color than mums and are easy to grow. The plant also provides a critical fall nectar source for pollinators, especially monarchs as the butterflies stock up for their fall migration to Mexico.

Above, Aromatic Aster, *S. oblongifolium*, grows in a neat, compact mound two- to four-feet tall and two- to three-feet wide. The New England Aster, *S. novae-angliae*, is taller, sometimes reaching five feet in height.

Plants can be cut back before July to improve their shape. Cutting back later will risk losing buds needed to produce flowers.

The plant is listed as one of the top twelve plants for butterflies.

Available from Good Nurseries
Size: 2-4 Feet Tall x 2-3 Feet Wide
Bloom: Blue, Purple, Pink, White / August to October
Uses: Borders, Massing, Naturalizing
USDA Zones: 4-8
Sun: Full Sun
Soil: Medium, Rich; Tolerates Clay

Tradescantia (various species)
SPIDERWORT

Spiderwort has delicate, blue-purple, three-petaled flowers that grow up to one-and-a-half-inches in diameter. Flowers bloom for only a day, but the buds will bloom in succession from May to July.

Dark-green, arching, grass-like leaves extend about a foot or two from the plant, which tends to grow in clumps. The Ohio Spiderwort, *T. Ohiensis*, is a larger plant, growing two to three feet in full sun to part shade and in dry soil. Spider Lily, *T. virginiana*, is smaller, growing more like one- to three-feet tall in part to full shade in clay soil. Many other species are available, offering a choice of sizes and a variety of purple-blue flowers. Spiderwort is an easily grown, resilient plant that does best in partial shade. It can cause an allergic reaction for cats and dogs.

Available from Native Plant Growers
Size: 1-3 Feet Tall x 12-18 Inches Wide
Bloom: Blue-Violet / May to July
Uses: Border, Naturalize, Shade Garden, Woodlands

USDA Zones: 4-9
Sun: Part Sun to Shade
Soil: Various, Moist to Dry

Verbena canadensis
HOMESTEAD VERBENA

An easily grown, low-spreading, perennial ground cover, Homestead Verbena grows thick enough to choke out weeds. Because of its attractive and long-blooming flowers, several cultivars have been introduced that offer more flower colors than often found in native plants. 'Homestead' is a pretty spectacular one, with show-stopping blooms all year long in exquisite deep purple, red, or pink. Purple is by far my favorite hue as it blends nicely with other blue and white bloomers and contrasts nicely with yellow and orange ones.

A common, easily found ornamental plant that should be used more often, I have never had any insect problems with it, although occasionally it will suffer some winter damage with a partial die-off. Verbena has historically been used as an ingredient for herbal teas.

Readily Available
Size: 6 Inches Tall x 18-24 Inches Wide
Bloom: Purple, Red, Pink, White / May to October
Uses: Containers, Ground Cover, Massing, Rock Gardens
USDA Zones: 6-10
Sun: Full Son
Soil: Dry to Medium Well-Drained

Verbesina encelioides
GOLDEN CROWNBEARD

Golden Crownbeard is one of the best nectar plants for bees, butterflies, and all kinds of insects. An annual, it is planted by seed and will reseed. It is often found on disturbed ground and along roadsides.

Crownbeard, also known as Cowpen Daisy, has yellow daisy-like flowerheads with gray-green toothed leaves. The plant is drought tolerant but will tend to flop or become messy with too much water or nutrients. Crownbeard is excellent for reclamation or disturbed areas and in pollinator conservation mixtures. Plant it by seed, but site it carefully as it will reseed prolifically. Plant seeds in November for following spring blooms.

Native Americans used the plant to treat skin ailments. A member of the aster family, it is also highly deer resistant.

Available from Native Seed Producers
Size: 1-3 Feet Tall x 1-3 Feet Wide
Bloom: Yellow / June to October
Uses: Accent, Ground Cover, Massing Naturalize
USDA Zones: 2-9
Sun: Full Sun
Soil: Sandy or Limestone, Alkaline

Gayfeather *(Liatris)*

Big Blue Stem *(Andropogon gerardii)*

Grasses

grasses: *vegetation consisting of typically short plants with long, narrow leaves.*

Grasses are green, nonwoody plants belonging to the grass family, the sedge family, or the rush family. Most grasses have round stems that are hollow between the joints, bladelike leaves, and an extensively branching fibrous root system.

In the ornamental landscape, grasses introduce exciting textures into the garden, along with movement and even sound as they rustle in the breeze.

You can select grasses in many hues, including dark burgundy, steely blue, white and green blends, gold, and bronzes.

The leaves often change colors during the growing season, shifting to rich, deeper shades in autumn followed by muted tones throughout the winter. The delicate seed heads of grasses in the landscape offer a whimsical accent to the landscape as well as value for livestock, including cattle, sheep, chickens, and pigs.

Andropogon gerardii
BIG BLUESTEM

One of the dominant grasses of the tallgrass prairie, Big Bluestem has attractive gray-to-blue-green foliage during the summer that takes on red tinges in the fall, and then after the frost, turns reddish bronze.

The flowers include distinct three-parted clusters that resemble turkey feet. A fine ornamental grass in dry areas, Big Bluestem has a root system that runs as much as seven- to eight-feet deep, and so it is tolerant of drought. If too much water is present, however, the plant will tend to fall over and lose its attractive vertical shape.

Big Bluestem is the larval host for many species of butterflies, and it is known as the "ice-cream grass" for livestock and wildlife because they often will eat it before any others. Both birds and mammals use Big Bluestem for nesting and cover in summer and winter.

Available from Native Plant Growers
Size: 4-6 Feet Tall x 2-3 Feet Wide
Bloom: Purplish Red / September to February
Uses: Accent, Massing, Back Border, Erosion Control
USDA Zones: 4-10
Sun: Full Sun
Soil: Tolerates All, Prefers Dry Infertile

Bouteloua curtipendula
SIDEOATS GRAMA

Sideoats Grama is a gray-green, clumping, warm-season grass that is also one of the toughest and showiest native grasses available. It is topped with slender, oatlike flowers that distinctly grace just one side of the stem; hence, the name "sideoats." In fall, the foliage and flowers turn rich shades of orange and bronze. A tough, deep-rooted grass, Sideoats Grama was once the main grass of the shortgrass prairie.

The grass has great potential in the ornamental landscape, and is one of the most important of range grass species—relished by livestock through the summer and fall. It is credited with helping the land recover after the Dust Bowl of the 1930s. Sideoats provides food for antelope and deer while growing, elk throughout the year, and wild turkeys during seeding.

Available from Native Plant Growers
Size: 18-24 Inches Tall x 12-18 Inches Wide
Bloom: Purplish-Tan / July to August
Uses: Borders, Erosion Control, Massing, Rocky Slopes

USDA Zones: 4-9
Sun: Full Sun
Soil: Any, Drought Tolerant

Bouteloua dactyloides
BUFFALO GRASS

Buffalo Grass is the grass that we should be using as a turfgrass in Oklahoma if we could go back in time before Bermuda grass invaded the United States. A low-growing, sod-forming, warm-season grass that will tolerate mowing, Buffalo Grass is incredibly drought tolerant, and will go dormant (but will not die) in the worst drought conditions. A gray-green, fine-textured grass, it was originally an instrumental part of the shortgrass prairie. It fares best in the dry western and central part of Oklahoma in clay soils. Because Buffalo Grass is slow to establish, it cannot compete with the aggressive Bermuda. To establish Buffalo Grass, the planting field must be completely cleared of the former, which is difficult to do. Buffalo can be seeded, although it is best planted by plugs at six to twelve inches on center. Several improved cultivars are available for better color.

Available from Some Sod Producers
Size: 4-6 Inches Tall
Bloom: Green, Not Showy / April to December
Uses: Accent, Ground Cover, Turfgrass

USDA Zones: 3-9
Sun: Full Sun
Soil: Prefers Slightly Clayey

Bouteloua gracilis
BLUE GRAMA

Blue Grama has a light blue-green, fine-textured foliage. Flowers are like horizontal eyelashes with a nice chartreuse color that ages to blonde seed heads in fall. The species can also be used as a weather-resistant, deep-rooted, warm-season turfgrass.

The cultivars, 'Blonde Ambition' and 'Hachita', are most showy and vigorous. They can reach thirty inches tall in bloom and perform excellently in an ornamental setting with showy flowers that compete with any ornamental alien grass. The blooms extend as much as a foot taller than the main plant and definitely show from a distance. Blue Grama's consistent size makes it great for massing, but it also makes a fine single accent plant. On the shortgrass prairie, Blue Grama rates with Buffalo Grass as one of the most important forage plants.

Available from Good Nurseries
Size: 8-30 Inches Tall x 24 Inches Wide
Bloom: White, Blonde / June to August
Uses: Accent, Filler, Lawns, Massing

USDA Zones: 3-10
Sun: Full Sun
Soil: Sand or Clay

Carex (various species)
SEDGES

There are more than five thousand species of grass-like or rush-like plants in the family *Cyperaceae* worldwide, and more than a hundred species of *Carex* or native Sedge that look and act like grasses. Sedge is found in many habitats—from sandy beaches to mountains to woodlands, swamps and marshes. The plants are versatile, especially as to size and leaf color, and far too diverse to cover in detail here.

I admit to not having had great success with Sedge. Still, I do see them doing well in other ornamental landscapes with irrigation, although it can take a couple of seasons for them to reach a usable size. Most Sedges do much of their growing in the cooler seasons, going dormant in hot temperatures. Native Americans used the leaves to make rope and both the leaves and rhizomes to make baskets, mats, and clothing.

Available from Good Nurseries   **USDA Zones:** 5-9
Size: 6 Inches to 6 Feet Tall   **Sun:** Part Sun to Shade
Bloom: Insignificant   **Soil:** Any, Long as Moisture
Uses: Ground Covers, Massing, Shade Gradens, Water Gardens   Present

Chasmanthium latifolium
NORTHERN SEA OATS

Northern Sea Oats is an attractive shade-loving grass that is native to streams and riverbanks but also tolerant of sea spray (the latter obviously not a problem in Oklahoma). The attractive foliage is similar to bamboo, and the seed heads rustle easily in the wind, adding movement to the garden. The flowers look like flat oats and emerge greenish-pink and then dry to a golden color, showy well into the winter months. When the seed heads get large, the plant will often flop over from the weight. Foliage turns coppery in fall and then brown in winter. Foliage should be sheared back in early spring to make way for new growth.

Northern Sea Oats will self-seed in moist soil, which is a good thing when used in the right location, but it can be problematic in manicured beds or near shaded lawns. It is drought and salt tolerant once established.

Available from Native Plant Growers
Size: 2-3 Feet Tall x 2 Feet Wide
Bloom: Pinkish to Gold / August to September
Uses: Accent, Ground Covers, Massing
USDA Zones: 4-9
Sun: Part Sun to Shade
Soil: Any, Long as Moisture Present

Eragrostis spectabilis
PURPLE LOVE GRASS

    A fine-textured, warm-season, bunch grass that loves sandy soils and full sun, Purple Love Grass is tough and drought tolerant, even growing under black walnut trees and near roadsides that receive winter road salt. Seed heads bloom midsummer with shades of purple, lending the landscape a reddish-purple haze as if clouds hovered above the ground.

    Planted by either seed or plugs, the perennial grass grows low to the ground in dense tufts; Purple Love Grass will self-seed and is best used in masses or naturalized settings. Eventually, the foliage breaks off and floats around like a tumbleweed. The plant is sometimes confused with Love Grass, *E. curvula*, which is taller but originates from southern Africa, and is not native to this region.

Available: Native Plant Growers or Seed Suppliers
Size: 1-2 Feet Tall x 1-2 Inches Wide
Bloom: Reddish-Purple / July to August
Uses: Massing, Naturalize, Rock Garden
USDA Zones: 5-9
Sun: Full Sun
Soil: Any but Prefers Dry Sandy or Gravelly

Muhlenbergia capillaris
PINK MUHLY GRASS

Muhly grasses offer stunning flowering accents for the warm season garden, with the bonus of Pink Muhly Grass being that it also attracts ladybugs. Many different cultivars exist, many of which are not cold-tolerant so be careful to pick a cultivar that is hardy for your area. There are taller species for background plantings and others that grow much lower for massing. Muhly has fine-textured, gray-green foliage that turns pink in the fall. The plant needs full sun and dry conditions to look its best, and may suffer in shade or during wet summers.

Rose Muhly, *M. reverchonii*, is shorter (twenty-four- to thirty-inches tall) with similar fall flowering. Pink Muhly Grass makes for an eye-popping addition to the garden and is drought tolerant too, although it can tolerate flooding for short spells.

Available from Good Nurseries
Size: 2-4 Feet Tall x 2-4 Feet Wide
Bloom: Purple-Pink or White / September to November
Uses: Accent, Borders, Massing, Meadows

USDA Zones: 5-9
Sun: Full Sun
Soil: Best in Sandy, Rocky, Well-Drained

Nassella tenuissima
MEXICAN FEATHER GRASS

Mexican Feather Grass is so widely available and widely used that I fear it has become significantly overused in Oklahoma landscapes. Yet there is no denying its appeal. The plant has a graceful, fine, hairlike texture that weeps to the ground, especially when flowering. The plant also boasts silky, golden flowers.

Feather grass offers a great contrast to any other plant, but it is best used in mass plantings and in areas where the seedlings can't spread to natural plant ecologies. That said, I won't plant this plant anymore. Mexican Feather Grass self-seeds to its detriment and spreads throughout cracks in concrete and anywhere else the seeds contact the ground. The grass has been classified as an invasive species in some regions. There are better grasses to use in your landscape that are less invasive and more beneficial for pollinators.

Readily Available
Size: 1-3 Feet Tall x 2 Feet Wide
Bloom: Silvery-White / June to September
Uses: Accent, Massing

USDA Zones: 5-10
Sun: Full Sun
Soil: Sandy, Clay, Average

Panicum virgatum
SWITCHGRASS

Distinguished by graceful, arching foliage, Switchgrass is an important species to plant along riverbanks and ponds, because its deep roots help to stabilize the banks. The plant can also tolerate the occasional flood. Away from water, Switchgrass makes for a well-mannered plant that will stay in place, becoming a thick clump of foliage. Hairy plumes of flowers top the foliage in the summer, turning into lacy seed heads. Summer color is usually blue-green, turning yellow-orange in the winter.

A drought-tolerant and adaptable grass with many uses in the landscape, Switchgrass can be encouraged to produce new growth by cutting clumps back in early spring. Cultivars have been named to distinguish shapes: 'Heavy Metal' is fat, 'Northwind' is taller and narrow, and 'Shenandoah' has a reddish hue.

Available from Good Nurseries
Size: 3-8 Feet Tall x 4 Feet Wide
Bloom: Pinkish / July to August
Uses: Accent, Borders, Detention Ponds, Massing, Screening

USDA Zones: 3-9
Sun: Full Sun to Part Sun
Soil: Dry to Wet, Prefers Moist Sandy, Clay

Schizachyrium scoparium
LITTLE BLUESTEM

Little Bluestem is the grass you see along roadways in Oklahoma and in places where no one mows or maintains the grass. It has a strict upright growth and thanks to its bluish color stands out in the summer and again come fall when it turns a salmon/copper color. While the stems of other grasses become matted in winter, the stems of Little Bluestem remain boldly upright; its roots can extend five to eight feet below ground.

Little Bluestem is drought tolerant and overall a tough plant. If Little Bluestem starts to slump, it is being overwatered or over fertilized. It actually thrives on neglect. 'Blaze' is a cultivar noted for its reddish fall and winter color. 'The Blues' is a compact cultivar with metallic blue foliage. The grass is deer resistant and provides nesting shelter for bees.

Available from Native Plant Growers
Size: 2-4 Feet Tall x 1 Foot Wide
Bloom: Green / July to September
Uses: Accent, Ground Cover, Massing

USDA Zones: 3-10
Sun: Full Sun to Part Sun
Soil: Any, Except Wet or Boggy

Sorghastrum nutans
INDIAN GRASS

Since January 24, 1972, Indian Grass has been the official state grass of Oklahoma, but for eons it was a major component of the North American tallgrass prairie. The grass grows in upright clumps with stiff, vertical flowering stems, topped with foot-long flower panicles that rise well above the foliage in the late summer. Indian Grass has blue-green foliage and is topped by showy, golden flower plumes. The foliage turns first yellow and then orange in the fall.

A striking grass for accent or massing and useful in erosion control, Indian Grass is perennial and also provides excellent wildlife habitat as well as food for deer. As with other native grasses, it is best to avoid too much irrigation or fertilization to ensure the best form. Some cultivars are available for improved color.

Available from Native Plant Growers
Size: 3-6 Feet Tall x 2-3 Feet Wide
Bloom: Golden / September to November
Uses: Accent, Back Border, Cut Flower, Massing

USDA Zones: 4-10
Sun: Full Sun to Part Sun
Soil: Any

Sporobolus heterolepis
PRAIRIE DROPSEED

Dropseed is a clump-forming, warm season grass native to the tallgrass prairie. It has fine-textured, medium-green leaves in an arching form, like a waterfall, before pink and brown-tinted flower heads emerge in mid to late summer. The foliage turns golden with orange hues in the fall, fading to light bronze. It is known for its airy flowers and seed heads.

The plant is known to be slow-growing and slow to establish, but once established Dropseed needs little care other than pulling, cutting, or burning off old foliage in late winter or early spring. However, I will admit I have not been successful with it. I may just be impatient, but in my landscape, the plant has only grown six inches in the first year, and I have yet to see its beautiful arching form, although I'm told it is particularly striking when positioned so the flower and seed heads are backlit.

Available from Native Plant Growers
Size: 2-3 Feet Tall x 2-3 Feet Wide
Bloom: Green/Pink/Copper / August to October
Uses: Ground Cover, Meadows, Rain Garden

USDA Zones: 3-9
Sun: Full Sun
Soil: Average to Well-Drained, Tolerates Clay

Tallgrass Prairie Preserve, near Pawhuska, Oklahoma

Native
Blue Grama

Native
Coreopsis

Blackfoot
Daisy

Like This, Plant This

*Study nature, love nature, stay close to nature.
It will never fail you.*
—**Frank Lloyd Wright**
American architect

Native Plants

I often hear people say they don't want to use native plants for fear the neighbors won't like it—or because it might look messy or violate their homeowner association guidelines. Nothing could be further from the truth. Using native plants in Oklahoma ornamental landscapes just means that instead of using plants from other parts of the world, we use native plants in an ornamental way.

What does that mean? It means that instead of using alien plants, basically plants not native to an ecosytem, you can use a native plant to achieve the same effect. Such as:

Traditional Alien Species	Consider this Native Plant
Mums (Asia, northeastern Europe)	Asters
Boxwood (Europe, Asia)	Amsonia
Moneywort (Europe)	Wild Strawberry
Autumn Joy Sedum (Europe, Asia)	Joe Pye Weed
Daylily (Asia)	Black-Eyed Susan
Rose (Asia)	Autumn Sage
Vinca (Europe, southern Russia)	Frogfruit
Fountain Grass (Africa)	Blonde Ambition Blue Grama
Maiden Grass (Asia)	Switchgrass
Feather Reed Grass (Europe, Asia)	Indian Grass

Many, many more native plants work equally well. Ideally, someday the whole landscape design process—which involves selection of plants to fit a location—will shift slightly so we consider native plants first when choosing plants for our homes and businesses.

Tall Garden Phlox *(Phlox paniculata)*

Preparing to Plant

Preparing the Planting Area

In Oklahoma, the greatest nuisance to any large planting project is Bermuda Grass. An invasive species brought here from Africa in the 1800s, it has been established as a major turfgrass in all parts of Oklahoma and the south, in full-sun landscapes. To prepare an area for planting, it is important to kill or remove the Bermuda Grass first. While organic ways exist to rid a site of Bermuda (solarization with plastic for one), I have yet to see it done successfully—usually it requires multiple applications of herbicide to create a clean growing area. Resist the urge to amend the soil. Rich soils tend to make native plants grow taller only to then flop over. It is important to plant most of these plants in early spring as the first flush of growth begins.

Plant Sizes

Most of the plants in this book are intended to be planted as container plants. One of the many great things about native plants is that you don't need to plant very large plants. A one-gallon plant will usually fill a spot in the first year. For ground covers, and for people who have more patience than I do, four-inch pots will work just fine.

Seeding

Another way to establish native plants is by seed. While slower, it is a less costly way to plant large areas. Preparation of the planting area remains important. Planting at the correct time of year (fall for annuals and perennials; spring for grasses) is vital. Be sure to plant seed at the proper depth and with good contact with the soil. Moisture is needed for germination and establishment. Locally sourced seed is more likely to adapt and recommended for better success.

Soil

Unsure if your soil is sandy, clay, or perfect loam? Here is a simple test: Wet your soil slightly, and then take a bit in your hand and roll it into a ball or ribbon. If it doesn't hold its shape, it is sandy. If it holds together nicely, it is clay. If it is somewhere in between, you are one of the lucky few with loamy soil.

Maintenance

A native landscape can be maintained much like any other landscape—with one major advantage—you don't have to water as much or as often! Most natives in this book are drought tolerant, although watering them may be needed to establish them. Still, more native plants are killed by overwatering than underwatering.

So when you're tempted to water your native plants, instead of doing it automatically, reach down and feel the ground to check the moisture level of the soil. Native plants are known for their deep root systems, often extending several feet down into the soil and providing access to water not available to other plants.

Watch plants carefully for the first couple of years. After that, they are best left alone. Most perennials and grasses will need to be cut back to the crown in the spring. Leave seed heads for birds to feast on during winter. Most natives do not need fertilization and *never* spray to kill insects, as this will also kill the pollinators our landscapes so desperately need.

Keeping the Neighbors Happy

I have often heard that one of the reasons people resist using native plants is that the neighbors will complain. If you have a messy, unkempt landscape, whether filled with natives or not, they probably have a right to do so. But a native plant landscape is not synonymous with a messy one. A few tips:

- Achieve a nicely designed landscape by using the same guidelines as you would with alien plants: Right plant—right place.
- Avoid the "messy" parts of native plants, by arranging them so the leggy parts are hidden by lower growing grasses or shorter plants.
- Combine plants with different flowering times so there is always something to look at.
- Keep edges neat! Use a mow strip, stone, or edging to define bed edges in a pleasant design. Keep the outside of those edges trimmed or mowed to contrast with the plants within the beds.

Joe Pye Weed (*Eutrochium purpureum*), with American goldfinch

Oklahoma Plant Chart

BOTANICAL NAME	COMMON NAME		PLANT HEI...

FORBS

Botanical Name	Common Name		
Achillea millefolium	Common Yarrow	●	●
Amorpha canescens	Leadplant		●
Amsonia hubrichtii	Arkansas Bluestar		●
Amsonia tabernaemontana	Bluestar		●
Aquilegia canadensis	Columbine	●	●
Aquilegia chysantha var. hinkleyana	Texas Gold Columbine	●	●
Asclepias syriaca	Common Milkweed		●
Asclepias tuberosa	Butterfly Weed	●	●
Asclepias viridis	Green Milkweed	●	●
Baptisia australis	Blue False Indigo		
Callirhoe involucrata	Purple Poppy Mallow	●	
Conoclinium coelestinum	Blue Mistflower	●	●
Coreopsis lanceolata	Lanceleaf Coreopsis	●	●
Coreopsis tripteris	Tall Coreopsis		
Coreopsis verticillata	Threadleaf Coreopsis	●	●
Dalea purpurea	Purple Prairie Clover	●	●
Echinacea purpurea	Purple Coneflower	●	●
Engelmannia pinnatifida	Engelmann's Daisy, Cutleaf Daisy		
Eryngium yuccifolium	Rattlesnake Master		
Eutrochium purpureum	Sweet Joe Pye Weed		
Fragaria virginiana	Wild Strawberry	●	
Gaillardia pulchella	Indian Blanket	●	●
Gaura lindheimeri	Gaura		●
Helianthus maximiliani	Maximilian Sunflower		
Heliopsis helianthoides	False Sunflower		●
Heuchera americana	Heuchera, Coral Bells	●	
Liatris (various species)	Blazing Star, Gayfeather		●
Lobelia cardinalis	Cardinal Flower		●
Malvaviscus arboreus	Turk's Cap		●
Melampodium leucanthum	Blackfoot Daisy	●	
Monarda fistulosa	Bee Balm		●

1 foot or less   1-3 feet   Over 3 feet   Full Sun 6+ hours   4-6 hours full sun, or dappled all day   Less than 4 hours, morning preference

88

	EXPOSURE			SOILS			POLLINATORS	

Soil, Sandy, Rocky	Medium Soil, Rich, Well-Drained	Wet Soil, Clay Or Holds Water	Attractive to Butterflies, Provides Food	Attractive to Birds, Provides Food

BOTANICAL NAME	COMMON NAME	PLANT HEIGHT	
FORBS continued			
Packera obovata	Golden Ragwort	●	●
Penstemon digitalis	Beard Tongue		●
Phlox divaricata	Wild Blue Phlox	●	
Phlox paniculata	Tall Garden Phlox		●
Phlox pilosa	Downy Phlox	●	
Phlox subulata	Creeping Phlox	●	
Phyla nodiflora	Frog Fruit	●	
Pycnanthemum tenuifolium	Slender Mountain Mint		●
Ratabida columnifera	Mexican Hat	●	●
Rudbeckia hirta	Black-Eyed Susan		●
Rudbeckia maxima	Giant Coneflower		
Rudbeckia submentosa	Sweet Coneflower		
Salvia greggii	Autumn Sage		●
Silphium perfoliatum	Cup Plant		
Solidago	Goldenrod		●
Symphyotrichum novae-angliae	New England Aster		
Symphyotrichum oblongifolium	Aromatic Aster		●
Tradescantia (various species)	Spiderwort	●	●
Verbena canadensis	Homestead Verbena	●	
Verbesina encelioides	Golden Crownbeard	●	●
GRASSES			
Andropogon gerardii	Big Bluestem		
Bouteloua curtipendula	Side Oats Grama	●	●
Bouteloua dactyloides	Buffalo Grass	●	
Bouteloua gracilis	Blue Grama	●	●
Carex (various species)	Sedges	●	●
Chasmanthium latifolium	Northern Sea Oats		●
Eragrostis spectabilis	Purple Love Grass		●
Muhlenbergia capillaris	Pink Muhly Grass		●
Nassella tenuissima	Mexican Feather Grass	●	●
Panicum virgatum	Switchgrass		
Schizachyrium scoparium	Little Bluestem		●
Sorghastrum nutans	Indian Grass		
Sporobolus heterolepis	Prairie Dropseed		●

1 foot or less   1-3 feet   Over 3 feet   Full Sun 6+ hours   4-6 hours full sun, or dappled all day   Less than 4 hours, morning preference

EXPOSURE				SOILS			POLLINATORS	
🌱	☀	✹	✷	💧	💧	💧	🦋	🐦
	●	●	●		●	●	●	
	●	●	●	●	●	●	●	●
		●	●		●	●	●	●
	●	●			●	●	●	●
	●	●		●	●		●	
	●	●		●	●		●	
	●	●		●	●	●	●	
	●	●		●	●		●	
				●				
●	●	●		●	●	●	●	●
●	●	●			●	●	●	●
●					●		●	●
●						●	●	●
●	●			●	●	●	●	
●	●			●	●	●	●	
●	●			●	●	●	●	
	●		●	●	●	●	●	
●				●			●	
●				●			●	●
				●		●	●	●
				●	●	●	●	
●				●	●	●		●
●				●	●	●	●	●
	●	●		●	●	●	●	●
	●	●		●	●	●	●	●
●				●	●	●	●	●
●				●				●
●				●	●	●		
●	●			●	●	●	●	●
●	●			●	●	●	●	●
●				●	●	●	●	●
●				●	●		●	●

💧	💧	💧	🦋	🐦
Soil ndy, Rocky	Medium Soil, Rich, Well-Drained	Wet Soil, Clay Or Holds Water	Attractive to Butterflies, Provides Food	Attractive to Birds, Provides Food

91

Pink Muhly Grass *(Muhlenbergia capillaris)*

Common Questions

*In the spring, at the end of the day,
you should smell like dirt.*

—Margaret Atwood
Novelist, Poet, Environmental Activist

Native Plants
Q & A

Question: What's difficult about landscaping with native plants?
Answer: Finding them! Luckily, several Oklahoma growers specialize in native plants, but due to the relatively low demand, they might not grow the variety and quantity to supply what is needed any given year. So, one year, you might fall in love with *Rudbeckia maxima*, and the next, you might not be able to find the plant for sale.

Question: How does a gardener deal with that?
Answer: You have to stay flexible. Be prepared to substitute similar plants. Or, order plants in advance. The likelihood of finding the plants you want improve if six months before spring you contact your favorite growers about what you want. That works best when needing a lot of plants, but it can help even the average gardener.

Question: What about ordering native plants by mail?
Answer: I encourage everyone to support local growers as a priority. We need them and want them to succeed and grow more natives. Years ago, I ordered plants through a catalog with a poor outcome. The plants arrived smaller than expected and in various degrees of vigor. But this past spring, I ordered some Indian Grass online. The plants arrived on time and in good health. They are smaller than I would have liked, which means they'll need more care at first. Don't, however, resort to catalog or online purchases just to save money. Order online only if plants cannot be found locally.

Question: How long does it take for native plants to make a statement in a landscape?
Answer: There's only one good answer to that question: It depends—mostly, on *when* you plant. The best time to plant is April to May as plants emerge from dormancy. You can expect to see an explosion of growth then and plants fill in quickly—sometimes in a matter of weeks. But don't space plants too far apart. The goal should be to have the ground covered by the end of the first year so weeds and Bermuda Grass won't find themselves welcome.

Question: What else should I know?
Answer: Some plants will spread, reseed, and take over other plants. Such traits are alluded to in our plant descriptions. But it can also happen with the alien plants we grew up with. You can either weed them out or learn to love them, depending on the plant and your personality. If you are a control freak, you may have a problem with some natives.

Question: Any more advice?
Answer: Yes, soil requirements are noted for each plant. This is more important on natives than a standard garden-center plant. If you have heavy red clay, you will have trouble growing something that wants well-drained soil. Remember to match the plant to the soil type.

Question: What about gathering native plants from the wild?
Answer: No! Transplanting plants with deep root systems is difficult and will often result in the death of the plant. It also robs the wild of native plants. Leave this work to professionals.

Question: Do I need to get rid of my non-native plants?
Answer: No—our goal is simply to encourage more people to use native plants as ornamentals. I am not about to remove all of my Nandina, Abelia, or the Japanese Boxwoods that have been growing on my property for years. Instead, I plant native plants in my new beds and use them to fill in around my old non-natives. If a plant dies, I look to native plant lists first to replace it.

Other Good Native Plants

*I love spring anywhere, but if I could choose
I would always greet it in a garden.*

—Ruth Stout
American gardening author

More Plants to Try

In this book, we have featured native plants that we have personally used in Oklahoma. Along the way, however, we also received recommendations about other native plants that local growers have seen fare well here. I am looking forward to trying them. Until then, we share some of those suggestions in the following list, with the hope that you'll let us know if you find them a good addition to the repertoire of Oklahoma native plants.

Coreopsis tinctora, Plains Coreopsis: Grows two to four feet tall with yellow rays surrounding a reddish-brown center from June to September. Grows in full sun but tolerates shade. Self-seeds readily.

Echinacea pallida, Pale Purple Coneflower: Needs well-drained soil and full to part sun. Grows to three feet tall with a pale purple flower.

Euphorbia marginata, Snow on the Mountain: An annual plant that I have seen growing in Oklahoma meadows. Admired for its showy leaf color, which has white on the leaf margins. The plant's sap is toxic if ingested.

Gaillardia aestivalis, Summer Gaillardia: Annual/perennial that blooms May to October with yellow rays. Fares best in full sun and dry soils.

Helianthus angustifolia, Swamp Sunflower: Perennial sunflower that boasts yellow flowers on six-foot-tall stems in full sun and wet or swampy soils.

Hibiscus laevis, Hardy Hibiscus: Beautiful hibiscus plant, with huge flowers, that suits wet soils in full sun. Plant can reach four to six feet in height.

Hymenoxys odorata, Bitter Rubberweed: An annual native to the dry western part of Oklahoma. Low growing with long blooming yellow flowers, it is poisonous to livestock and sheep.

Monarda bradburyana, Eastern Beebalm: Plant has similar growth culture and flower as the *Monarda fistulosa* but is lower growing—only one to two feet tall and blooms in May.

Parthenium integrifolium, Wild Quinine: Four feet tall with cauliflower-looking white flowers from June through September, it grows in full sun, in sandy and rocky soils, and is very drought tolerant.

Phlox stolonifera, Creeping Phlox: The plant looks very much like the *Phlox subulata* but has purple flowers and grows in shade.

Polygonatum biflorum, Solomon's Seal: A graceful, low-growing plant for use in full to partial shade. I've grown Variegated Solomon Seal for years, but it is not a native. If you can find this plant, get it!

Rivina humilis, Pigeonberry: Another low-growing ground cover for the shady places in your landscape.

Salvia azurea var. grandiflora, Blue Sage: Herbaceous perennial that grows to be five feet tall with blue flowers. Blooms from July to October.

Sautellaria incana, Scullcap. With blue flowers from July to September, it grows two to three feet tall and tolerates dry and clay soils.

Verbesina alternifolia, Wingstem: Easy to grow from seed, this native plant grows four to eight feet tall with yellow blooms from August to October. It can be somewhat weedy but is good for naturalizing.

Vernonia lettermannii, Narrowleaf Ironweed. A very tough plant with strong stems, Narrowleaf Ironweed can grow four to six feet tall with red or purple blooms from July through September. It does well in moist to average soils for borders, rain gardens, or naturalized situations.

Verbena stricta, Hoary Vervain: Easily grown from seed and drought tolerant, this plant will also self-seed. It grows to be two to four feet tall and has blue-purple flowers from May to September.

Where to See Native Plants

*To make a prairie it takes a clover and one bee,
one clover, and a bee, and revery.
The revery alone will do if bees are few.*

—Emily Dickinson,
American poet

Native Plant Destinations

Native plants grace public spaces across Oklahoma, providing gardeners the opportunity to see the plants used as ornamentals in various settings both informal and formal, residential and commercial. Here are a few places to see native plants in Oklahoma at their best, including one where they still grow wild.

Oklahoma City

Myriad Botanical Gardens, *301 W. Reno Avenue, Oklahoma City, OK 73102, (405) 445-7080*

Oklahoma City Zoo and Botanical Garden, *2101 N.E. Fiftieth Street, Oklahoma City, OK 73111, (405) 424-3344*

Will Rogers Garden, *Will Rogers Park, 3400 N.W. Thirty-Sixth Street, Oklahoma City, OK 73112, (405) 297-1392*

Kirkpatrick Garden at OSU-OKC, *400 N. Portland Avenue, Oklahoma City, OK 73107, (405) 945-3350*

Martin Park Nature Center, *5000 W. Memorial Road, Oklahoma City, OK 73142, (405) 297-1429*

Scissortail Park (Grand Opening in September 2019; scheduled for completion in 2021), *300 S.W. Seventh Street, Oklahoma City, OK 73109, (405) 445-7080*

Tulsa

The Gathering Place, *2650 S. John Williams Way E., Tulsa, OK 74114, (918) 779-1000*

Tulsa Botanic Garden, *3900 Tulsa Botanic Drive, Tulsa, OK 74127, (918) 289-0330*

Woodward Park, *2435 S. Peoria Avenue, Tulsa, OK 74114, (918) 576-5155*

Stillwater

The Botanic Garden at Oklahoma State University, *3300 W. Sixth Street, Stillwater, OK 74078, (405) 744-5404*

Pawhuska

Tallgrass Prairie Preserve (largest tract of remaining tallgrass prairie in the world), *15316 County Road 4201, Pawhuska, OK 74056, (918) 287-4803*

Poteau

The Kerr Center for Sustainable Agriculture, *24456 Kerr Road, Poteau, OK 74953, (918) 647-9123*

Glossary

American Society of Landscape Architects: founded in 1899, professional association representing landscape architects around the world.

alien: non-native plant that may cause environmental harm or adversely impact biodiversity, including the decline or elimination of native species.

annual: a plant that completes its life cycle within one year, and then dies.

clay soil: soil with a high amount of clay, which sticks together when compressed, lacks oxygen, and fails to easily absorb water.

cultivar: plant variety produced in cultivation by selective breeding for developing special characteristics (flowering, fruiting, size).

deadheading: to pinch or remove dead or faded flowers from plants, commonly done to increase flowering or improve appearance.

enriched soil: high quality garden soil that has been enriched with compost, organic nutrients.

foliage: the aggregate of leaves of one or more plants.

herbaceous: plants, or herbs, that have no persistent woody stem.

invasive plant: a plant that is both non-native and able to establish on many sites, grows quickly, and spreads to the point of disrupting plant communities or ecosystems.

legume: a family of plants with the ability to harvest nitrogen gas from the air and combine it with hydrogen, producing a form of nitrogen that can improve the soil and provide supplemental nitrogen to nearby plants.

mulch: a layer of organic material spread over the surface of soil to reduce evaporation, control weeds, regulate temperature, enrich soil, reduce erosion, and add beauty.

nativar: a cultivar of a native plant, generally done to select for improved flowering, color, or other growth characteristics.

native plant: a plant that is a part of the balance of nature having developed for hundreds or thousands of years in a particular region or ecosystem.

naturalized: a non-native plant that does not need human help to reproduce and maintain itself over time in an area where it is not native.

perennial: a plant that persists for many growing seasons. Generally, top portion of plant dies back each winter, and plant regrows the following spring from the same root system. Some perennials do keep their leaves year-round and make for attractive borders or ground covers.

pollination: the transfer of pollen between the male and female parts of flowers to enable fertilization and reproduction. Most plants depend on pollinators to transfer pollen.

pollinators: a group of animals—especially bees, flies, wasps, butterflies, moths, beetles, weevils, ants, midges, bats, and birds—that serve to pollinate plants.

rhizome: a continuously growing horizontal underground stem that sends out lateral shoots at intervals, allowing plants to spread.

Registered Landscape Architect (RLA): a landscape architect that has taken and passed the Landscape Architect Registration Examination and is licensed by the state to practice landscape architecture.

sedge: a grasslike plant with triangular stems and inconspicuous flowers.

shrub: a small- to medium-sized woody plant; unlike herbaceous plants, shrubs will have woody stems above the ground.

species: a group of related organisms that share common characteristics and are capable of interbreeding.

tap root: a straight tapering root growing vertically downward and forming the center from which subsidiary rootlets spring.

weed: a native or non-native plant that is not valued where it is growing.

Acknowledgments

This book was made more accurate and comprehensive with the help of the following individuals. They are all specialists in the growth and use of native plants in Oklahoma. Their review, personal insight, and experience has been invaluable: Susan, who grows as many natives as possible on her acreage in eastern Oklahoma County (Susan is also a landscape professional focusing on native plants); Steve Dobbs, director of Landscape Services, Oklahoma State University, Stillwater, Oklahoma; Laurie Effinger, a seventeen-year veteran of the Oklahoma Department of Transportation Beautification Office where she supervised the planting of wildflowers across Oklahoma's state highway system; Bill Farris, Prairie Wind Nursery, Norman, Oklahoma, *prairiewindnursery.com*; and Marilyn Stewart, Wild Things Nursery, Seminole, Oklahoma, *wildthingsnursery.com*.

Tallgrass Prairie Preserve, near Pawhuska, Oklahoma

Resources

All gardening is landscape painting.
—William Kent, English architect

We wish to thank the following organizations and individuals for providing information and images for this book.

LADY BIRD JOHNSON WILDFLOWER CENTER
4801 La Crosse Avenue, Austin, TX 78739 | (512)-232-0100
www.wildflower.org

MISSOURI BOTANICAL GARDEN
4344 Shaw Boulevard, Saint Louis, MO 63110 | (314)-577-5100
www.missouribotanicalgarden.org

NOBLE RESEARCH INSTITUTE
2510 Sam Noble Parkway, Ardmore, OK 73401 | (580)-223-5810
www.noble.org

PHOTOGRAPHERS
Illinois botanist and photographer Chris Benda
Oklahoma photographers Laurie Effinger and Harvey Payne

PLANT DATABASES
*www.illinoisbotanizer.com, www.oklahomaplantdatabase.org,
www.plants.usda.gov, www.nrcs.usda.org*

Other helpful references include:
KERR CENTER FOR SUSTAINABLE AGRICULTURE
24456 Kerr Road, Poteau, OK 74953 | (918) 647-9123
www.kerrcenter.com

OKIES FOR MONARCHS
www.okiesformararchs.org

Common Name Index

FORBES

Aromatic Aster 61
Autumn Sage 58
Beard Tongue 47
Bee Balm 45
Black-Eyed Susan 55
Blackfoot Daisy 44
Blazing Star, Gayfeather 41
Blue False Indigo 24
Blue Mistflower 26
Bluestar 19
Butterfly Weed 22
Cardinal Flower 42
Columbine 20
Common Milkweed 21
Creeping Phlox 51
Cup Plant 59
Downy Phlox 50
Engelmann's Daisy 32
False Sunflower 39
Frogfruit 52
Gaura 37
Giant Coneflower 56
Golden Crownbeard 64
Golden Ragwort 46
Goldenrod 60
Green Milkweed 23
Heuchera, Coral Bells 40
Homestead Verbena 63
Indian Blanket 36
Lanceleaf Coreopsis 27
Leadplant 18
Maximilian Sunflower 38
Mexican Hat 54
Purple Coneflower 31
Purple Poppy Mallow 25

Purple Prairie Clover 30
Rattlesnake Master 33
Slender Mountain Mint 53
Spiderwort 62
Sweet Coneflower 57
Sweet Joe Pye Weed 34
Tall Coreopsis 28
Tall Garden Phlox 49
Threadleaf Coreopsis 29
Turk's Cap 43
Wild Blue Phlox 48
Wild Strawberry 35
Yarrow, Common Yarrow 17

GRASSES

Big Blue Stem 68
Blue Grama 71
Buffalo Grass 70
Indian Grass 79
Little Bluestem 78
Mexican Feather Grass 76
Northern Sea Oats 73
Pink Muhly Grass 75
Prairie Dropseed 80
Purple Love Grass 74
Sedges 72
Sideoats Grama 69
Switchgrass 77

Scientific Name Index

FORBES

Achillea millefolium 17
Amorpha canescens 18
Amsonia (various species) 19
Aquilegia canadensis 20
Asclepias syriaca 21
Asclepias tuberosa 22
Asclepias viridis 23
Baptisia australis 24
Callirhoe involucrata 25
Conoclinium coelestinum 26
Coreopsis lanceolata 27
Coreopsis tripteris 28
Coreopsis verticillata 29
Dalea purpurea 30
Echinacea purpurea 31
Engelmannia pinnatifida 32
Eryngium yuccifolium 33
Eutrochium purpureum 34
Fragaria virginiana 35
Gaillardia pulchella 36
Gaura lindheimeri 37
Helianthus maximiliani 38
Heliopsis helianthoides 39
Heuchera americana 40
Liatris (various species) 41
Lobelia cardinalis 42
Malvaviscus arboreus 43
Melampodium leucanthum 44
Monarda fistulosa 45
Packera obovata 46
Penstemon digitalis 47
Phlox divaricata 48
Phlox paniculata 49
Phlox pilosa 50
Phlox subulata 51

Phyla nodiflora 52
Pycnanthemum tenuifolium 53
Ratabida columnifera 54
Rudbeckia hirta 55
Rudbeckia maxima 56
Rudbeckia submentosa 57
Salvia greggii 58
Silphium perfoliatum 59
Solidago (various species) 60
Symphyotrichum (various species) 61
Tradescantia (various species) 62
Verbena canadensis 63
Verbesina encelioides 64

GRASSES

Andropogon gerardii 68
Bouteloua curtipendula 69
Bouteloua dactyloides 70
Bouteloua gracilis 71
Carex (various species) 72
Chasmanthium latifolium 73
Eragrostis spectabilis 74
Muhlenbergia capillaris 75
Nassella tenuissima 76
Panicum virgatum 77
Schizachyrium scoparium 78
Sorghastrum nutans 79
Sporobolus heterolepis 80

About the Authors

Connie Scothorn

Connie Scothorn founded CLS & Associates in 1999 in Oklahoma City, Oklahoma. A licensed landscape architect, Scothorn is a member of the American Society of Landscape Architects. She also holds a bachelor's degree in horticulture-landscape design from Oklahoma State University.

Brian Patric

In 2010, Brian Patric joined CLS & Associates. He is now a partner in the firm. Patric holds a degree in landscape architecture from Oklahoma State University. This is Scothorn and Patric's first book.

About CLS & Associates

An award-winning landscape architecture firm based in Oklahoma City, Oklahoma, CLS & Associates celebrated its twentieth anniversary in 2019. The firm engages in a variety of projects, including streetscape development, parks, playgrounds, and recreational design, as well as landscape projects of all sizes. The use of native plants to improve aesthetic and ecological benefits to all landscaped sites has become a foundation of CLS's design principles. Visit its website: *www.clsokc.com*.